ARIZONA
HIGHWAYS

Indian Arts and Crafts

Edited by Clara Lee Tanner

Cover photo by Jerry Jacka

Published by **Arizona Highways**
2039 West Lewis Avenue, Phoenix, Arizona 85009 U.S.A.
James E. Stevens, Director of Publications.
Tom C. Cooper, Editor.
Wesley Holden, Associate Editor
Typography by Morneau Typographers, Phoenix.
Printed by W. A. Krueger Co., Phoenix.
Designed by Steve R. Losey, Tucson.

Contents

Preface

by Clara Lee Tanner

Events of a great drama over uncounted aeons were staged by nature in the creation of the wild, sweeping beauty found in the semi-arid region now encompassed by the states of Arizona, Colorado, New Mexico, and Utah. Primitive hunters and gatherers, living between two thousand and ten thousand years ago in what is now the American Southwest, left evidence of their creativeness in the baskets, rabbit-fur blankets, jewelry, tools, and weapons which have been unearthed. The gatherers are believed to have been sufficiently experienced with plants to adapt corn to successful cultivation; a firm base of agriculture led them to the sedentary life they developed prior to 300 B.C. and continued until the arrival of the Europeans in the sixteenth century.

Three major cultures evolved in this part of the United States. In southern Arizona were the Hohokam, parent culture to historic Pima and Papago. Today's Four Corners region was home to the colorful Anasazi People, ancestors of the contemporary Puebloans. The Mogollon culture of southwestern New Mexico is believed to have contributed some bloodlines to certain Puebloan groups of the Rio Grande valley. Further, these prehistoric peoples left a rich heritage in basketry, ceramics, and other crafts and their technologies.

A group of Athapascans from the north (not part of these three prehistoric cultures) drifted into the Southwest several centuries before the first-coming Spaniards. Eventually evolving into two distinct tribes, these latecomers came to be known as Apache and Navajo. Then came the Conquistadores in 1540, and the Spanish settlers in 1598, and later, Mexicans. New ways of living were introduced and taken up by the Indians. Political rule of the ancient lands was taken first by the Spaniards, then the Mexicans, and finally by the Anglo-Americans from beyond the plains; it was by these last that many of the Native Americans were placed on "reservations," beginning in 1859. Much of the Indian culture survived, particularly in religious and social expressions.

All of the craft arts which sustained the Indian throughout the centuries of their development were perpetuated historically. Certainly changes have been made, for any art is dead which does not change. Each of the crafts has known periods of development and periods of retrogression. Historically these have been tied in largely with the contact situation. Those cultures which retained more of their native aspects tended to continue with craft production; too, where commerce has been strong, crafts have not only survived but often have thrived. For example, because the Hopi used native baskets — particularly for ceremonial purposes — this craft remains alive to this day. Among the Papago, on the other hand, use of native basketry ceased

v

after the turn of this century, but at the same time Anglos became interested in them, so the craft has continued.

The period from the late 1960's to the mid 70's represents one of the most unusual times in the history of Indian art in the Southwest. Interest in the native American was accelerated as a result of national attitudes toward minority people. Too, more public interest was centered on Indian arts and crafts through exhibits and books and articles on the subject. America's tendency toward fadism began to flourish, and soon Indian arts and crafts were *the* thing. Sad results of the avid interest are reflected in rapidly and poorly produced crafts, more unqualified Indians producing crafts, and many non-Indians and even foreigners making objects. These comments apply to silver and jewelry almost exclusively.

Despite these undesirable trends there are now many fine Indian craftsmen producing excellent works of high artistic value. The Hopi and other tribal guilds, as well as dealers and individual Indian craftsmen, have been influential in keeping quality. When the smoke clears, there will still be fine Southwest Indian Art.

A look into the background of the chapter authors will indicate their qualifications for writing in the field of Southwestern Indian craft arts.

Jerold Collings is a prime authority on Indian baskets. Born on the California side of the Colorado River near Parker, Arizona, young Collings was taught Indian basketry art by Chemehuevi Indians before he was twelve. Since then he has continued to apprentice with weavers from almost every tribe in the Southwest. A graduate (in anthropology) of California State College at Long Beach, Collings is director of the Gila River Indian Arts and Crafts Center, on the reservation at Sacaton, Arizona. Himself a discriminating collector, Collings has judged many major Indian arts and crafts shows, and is highly respected by Indian craftsmen, peers in his profession, and collectors.

Joe Ben Wheat, with a doctorate in anthropology from the University of Arizona, has pursued archaeology in the Southwest and in Mexico, Tunisia, and the Republic of the Sudan. He made a study of regional museum collections of Southwestern ethnographic materials when he became curator of anthropology at the University of Colorado Museum in 1953. This culminated in a one-year sabbatical during which he analyzed and photographed about 3,000 pieces of Indian and Spanish-American textiles in European and American museums and archives.

As a result of continuing field research, Dr. Wheat has published several monographs and numerous articles on archaeology. His pursuit of textile studies has resulted in several significant publications on Navajo weaving. Dr. Wheat lives in Boulder, Colorado.

Barton Allen Wright is a graduate of the University of Arizona, with bachelor's and master's degrees in anthropology. He says he is "a hybrid archaeologist/artist," an apt title, for he has had a wealth of formal training and practical experience in both fields. For the past 20 years he has been involved in Hopi ". . . ceremonies and dances, births and deaths, marriages and mishaps," and, with his usual modesty, adds that he feels that he has "just arrived at the threshold of learning something about the Hopi." In reality, Wright has become *the* authority on Hopi kachinas. A firm foundation was laid for this in his working for some years at the Museum of Northern Arizona with Jimmie Kewanwytewa, a Hopi Indian from whom he acquired a vast knowledge about kachinas. Wright became curator at the Museum in 1958. He has judged many shows, has illustrated both archaeological and ethnological reports, and has published a number of books, particularly on the subjects of kachinas and kachina dolls.

Richard L. Spivey in a very short time achieved the distinction of being the undisputed authority on contemporary Pueblo Indian pottery, and an often quoted expert.

Spivey has a Stanford degree in economics, ten years' experience as part owner and general manager of a successful restaurant chain, and a compelling urge to devote himself to art. After moving to Santa Fe, Mr. Spivey was befriended by Popovi Da, famed potter from San Ildefonso, who had long recognized the need for solid business management and an aesthetic appreciation for Pueblo potters, and urged Spivey to combine these roles.

Since then he has made a lasting impact in the contemporary pottery market, not only in fair pricing and fair income for the potters, but in the quality of the production and the expansion of the market. Along the way he has gained an unprecedented knowledge and respect for the potters and their techniques.

Mr. Spivey has served as judge of Pueblo Indian pottery at the prestigious SWAIA Santa Fe Indian Market and at the Northern Pueblo Artists and Craftsmen show. He is currently serving his second term as president of the Southwestern Association on Indian Affairs, and has acted as consultant on Indian art to major cultural institutions.

David L. Neumann studied at Columbia University and the state universities of Michigan and Wisconsin, and at the Academy Julien in Paris. He visited Santa Fe in 1928, returning there to live in 1930, when he began his trading in Southwest Indian art, particularly on the Navajo Reservation. Between 1932 and 1945 he also did much traveling in Mexico, importing Mexican crafts into the United States for sale. From 1930 to the present Neumann has been a wholesale dealer of Indian handcrafts, particularly in Navajo and Zuni silverwork.

Robert Ashton was a major in anthropology at the University of Colorado; he also worked at the Colorado Museum. He spent many years as a range archaeologist at Mesa Verde National Park, and a year at Calico Hills, California, with the renowned Dr. L. S. B. Leakey. Interest in Indian art through these years culminated with active trading in 1967, and then the opening of a shop in Taos, New Mexico in 1971.

Sharon Ashton developed a feeling and understanding for Indian art and culture as she grew up in the Southwest. After graduating from the University of Arizona she moved to Kansas City, Missouri, where she opened an Indian shop.

Bob and his wife, Sharon, established the Ashton Gallery in Scottsdale, Arizona. Ashton inaugurated the Denver American Indian Art Show, and, with Sharon, started the Beverly Hills American Indian Art Show. The Ashtons have judged many Indian art shows in addition to their work as Indian art dealers, consultants, and appraisers. They are editors and publishers (with Hubert Guy) of *American Indian Art* magazine.

Foreword

With the possible exception of the commerce that must have taken place in the splendorous markets found by the Conquistadores in the sixteenth century in the great cities of the Americas, there never has occurred such a brisk trade in arts and crafts as that now being enjoyed by Native American artists and craftsmen. Today, American Indian arts and crafts products move vigorously through the most sophisticated of marketing channels, with sales figures running impressively into the millions of dollars.

The appreciation of Indian arts and crafts is no longer limited to the social scientist's scholarly interest in a traditional costume, blanket, basket, or ceremonial object produced originally for the use of tribal members. It now extends to a world-wide public whose attention is focused on a wide array of goods produced expressly for a non-Indian market. This assiduous regard for Indian arts and crafts stands in startling contrast to the attitude prevalent in the not-too-distant past when the creative expressions of the native peoples were viewed for the most part as attractive by-products of a quaint culture, rather than as works of art.

That it took so long for Indian art to attract such a widespread and rapt audience as now exists can be attributed in part to the function of art within the historic framework of Native American culture. For thousands of years aesthetic expression was so inextricably interwoven into the fabric of daily life of the native people that they did not consider it a singular activity. Objects were fashioned to meet utilitarian needs or to fulfill the requirements of ritual and religion, but rarely was their creation pursued as "art for art's sake." Indeed, most tribes had no equivalent in their language for the word *art*. Yet, art has served since antiquity as the primary instrument for the articulation of Native American culture and its evolution.

Of all the changes affecting Indian arts and crafts since the turn of this century, perhaps the most significant has been the development of new concepts and experimental directions, giving rise to questions regarding the validity of artistic expressions that veer from pure Indian tribal tradition. From a social caldron bubbling with an admixture of Indian nationalism and cultural transition, there has emerged a new breed of Indian artist and craftsman who would be hard put to ignore the implications of modern technology, tools, and materials.

These young artists and craftsmen, themselves products of a new age, not only see a world different than that of their forefathers, they see it through different eyes. Their artistic expressions reflect the condition of their environment as they perceive it to be. Just as the ancients created aesthetic forms in keeping with the nature of their times, so the young people of today are mirroring their view of the world around them. Thus are new traditions born.

But the new does not invalidate the old; nor vice versa. Each is a statement in its own right. Today, art forms grown of ancient tribal traditions flourish side by side with new forms that spring from a lively contemporary movement in which individual creativity is a dynamic force. Whatever form it may take, Indian art will be Indian art for so long as it is rooted in the realities of a distinctive Indian culture.

The success presently being enjoyed by Indian artists and craftsmen could not have been realized without the aggressive support of many friendly individuals and sponsoring institutions. ARIZONA HIGHWAYS stands high on the list of such contributors. This book, the work of specialists in five major areas of Indian arts and crafts: ceramics, jewelry, basketry, textiles, and katchina dolls, has been ably edited by Clara Lee Tanner whose love and support for American Indians and their arts have been affirmed through her own writings and her long-time identification as a scholar of Southwest Indian culture. This publication serves to reinforce the love affair that ARIZONA HIGHWAYS has been sponsoring for many years between its readers and an unbelievably handsome country, its mountains and rivers and deserts, its flora and fauna, and the accomplishments of *all* its people.

Lloyd Kiva New
Director, Institute of American Indian Arts;
Chairman, Indian Arts and Crafts Board,
U.S. Department of the Interior.

1/Basketry

by Jerold L. Collings

For at least the past 8,000 years, Native Americans inhabiting the Southwest have been producing basketry in a variety of forms and with considerable diversification of technique. Rigid and semirigid containers, mats, and bags — all played an important role in man's early attempts to cope with this strikingly beautiful, but often harsh, environment. It is of interest to note that even in the earliest known Southwestern occupation where basketry is found in definite association, the Desha Complex (dated about 5500–6000 B.C.), fragments of both close coiling and close twining were found. These techniques are the two most frequently used by basket weavers of the Southwest today. A third technique, plaiting, seems to be considerably later and it apparently never achieved the popularity enjoyed by coiling and twining. The most common form of plaited basket was a shallow bowl, usually of twill plaiting, formed by enclosing a wooden ring by the plaiting at the rim (Fig. 1.2). Baskets that are practically identical to those of 1,500 years ago are still being made by present day Hopi and Jémez weavers.

Archaeological evidence clearly establishes the prehistoric existence of the three major subclasses of basketry: twining, coiling, and plaiting. The twining subclass of basketry techniques are those weaves accomplished by passing moving horizontal elements (wefts) around stationary vertical elements (warps). In the coiling subclass of basketry weaves, moving vertical elements are sewn around stationary horizontal elements. In the third subclass, plaiting, all the elements are active, and pass over and under each other without any engagement. While all three of these basic techniques have been used extensively throughout the Southwest, and over long periods of time, the coiling technique has emerged as the most important tradition in Southwestern basketry. Not only does this method produce strong, durable, and very closely stitched basketry, but it offers the greatest potential for design development.

The coming of the historic period brought with it many changes in the life style of the native population. All areas of the Southwest were not affected equally or during the same period. Ultimately,

1.2 Plaited "ring baskets," like the one being completed by this Hopi weaver, have been made for at least 1500 years.
WESLEY HOLDEN

however, all of the native population underwent a cultural reassignment. Throughout much of this period (even into the early years of this century), Indian tradition was viewed as an obstacle to progress, and every available means was used to destroy it thoroughly and forever. While the ever-practical White man was quick to accept the native methods of utilizing the material resources of the Southwest, some found the cultural achievements to be contemptible. The Indian's arts and crafts were considered by many to be the survivals of a barbaric age.

Despite efforts to the contrary, a good deal of excellent basketry was produced throughout most of the historic period and in a few instances, it is still being made today. This is especially true of the Indians of Arizona, for it is among them that Southwestern basketry reaches its highest level of sophistication.

The traditional basket weaver was a true folk artist. She created works that were always an inextricable part of the social, economic, and ceremonial activities of her society. She worked within a limited range of shapes and designs that has been collectively established by the society of which she was a member. Yet, even working within these culturally imposed limitations, there was room for a high degree of individual achievement, and seemingly endless variation. It is probable that only an occasional, especially gifted individual would add her own contribution of talent or quality to the prevailing style. Thus, a new standard might be established that would become a model to be imitated by other weavers who though perhaps less gifted, were nonetheless strongly motivated to put forth their best effort. The effect was cumulative and resulted in the creation of basketry that both technically and aesthetically rivals the best done anywhere in the world.

While it is recognized that the preceding introduction has been brief and sketchy at best, it is hoped that even this small measure of background will contribute to the understanding and appreciation of the basketry produced in the past, as well as that which is produced in the Southwest at present. The subsequent discussion will deal primarily with the individual tribes that, in the recent past, have excelled in the art of basketry, or are now actively producing.

Western Apache

The Western Apache are divided into 5 groups, the White Mountain, Cibeque, San Carlos, Southern Tonto, and Northern Tonto. There is no evidence of Apache in Arizona prior to the middle of the 16th century. However, after the horse was introduced into the Southwest by the Spanish, the Apache became notorious raiders. From their mountain strongholds, they made frequent forays among the Pimans and Puebloans, and occasionally pillaged villages in the Mexican states of Sonora and Chihuahua. By the time the United States acquired Arizona as a result of the war with Mexico, the Apache had developed a "raiding economy." During the 1870's and 80's the Western Apache were at almost constant war with U.S. military forces, but by 1890 nearly all were peacefully settled on reservations in Arizona.

Because of their roving life, the Apache had few possessions. Their arts and crafts were limited mainly to basketry and the dressing of buckskin. They did not weave blankets, and produced only a small amount of rather crude pottery that was strictly utilitarian.

As basket makers, the Western Apache women more than made up for any shortcomings they may have had in the other arts and

crafts. While they practiced both close twining and close coiling, it is the latter technique in which the Western Apache truly excelled. Shallow bowls and olla shapes are the forms most commonly constructed in this technique. Bowls are typically between two and four inches in depth, and between twelve and sixteen inches in diameter. This is the size range most suited to such household uses as mixing, winnowing, parching, serving, and temporary storage. Around the turn-of-the-century, and later, outside demand inspired the production of some much larger baskets. Shallow bowls ranging from 20 to 30 inches in diameter, and often of superior workmanship, are known from this period (Fig. 1.3).

Apache basketry olla sizes tended to be quite large. Most are between 15 and 24 inches in height, although larger and smaller examples are not uncommon. These baskets required not only a great deal of time to construct (often a year or more), but also demanded the highest level of weaving competence to produce (Fig. 1.4).

Both the bowls and coiled ollas are constructed of willow or cottonwood, which provides the light colored background, and devil's-claw, which is used for the black design. Three rods (two on the bottom and one on top) form the foundation about which the stitches are sewn. The work direction is nearly always to the left. A reddish brown material prepared from the root of the yucca is used occasionally, and, in some instances, provides spectacular results. This trait seems to be quite

1.4 This Western Apache storage basket is 20½ inches tall, and is an outstanding example of the integration of zoomorphic, anthropomorphic, and geometric design elements.
JERRY JACKA
Heard Museum Collection

late, and judging from the relative scarcity of existing polychrome specimens, it seems never to have met with great favor among the weavers.

Western Apache basket designs are as varied as the land these people roamed. They range from extremely simple, static motifs, to complex arrangements in which a feeling of rapid whirling motion is conveyed. Since the very latter part of the 19th century, Western Apache weavers have been especially fond of life forms. Men, women, horses, dogs, deer, and birds are the ones most commonly used, but even exotic circus animals have found their much altered likenesses cleverly adapted to conform to Apache aesthetics, and the technical limitations of the three rod coiling technique. These life forms are often used to fill space within (or in conjunction with) geometric design elements (Fig. 1.5), but occasionally a basket is seen in which a more or less random arrangement of these figures constitutes the sole ornamentation.

If Western Apache basket designs ever had any significance beyond ornamentation, this has been lost. When asked to interpret the meaning of the designs on a basket, a typical reply is, "They make the basket look pretty." She might then add that she uses these designs "Because the old people used them."

In addition to the close coiled baskets, the Western Apache also make two types of baskets in the close twining technique — carrying baskets and water jars (Fig. 1.8). Some carrying baskets are more

5

or less conical in shape, but with a rounded bottom; others are bucket shaped. Several twining variations are employed, and occasionally occur in the same basket. The materials used vary from area to area, but willow and devil's-claw were commonly used in the San Carlos area, while wild mulberry and devil's-claw were often used in the finer burden baskets of the White Mountain Apache.

Burden basket designs are limited to simple horizontal bands usually executed in black and red. The black is devil's-claw and the red is most often obtained by dying some of the weft material, or by painting the design on the completed basket; it is then further decorated with buckskin fringe, to which beads and tin cones are sometimes attached.

Most Apache burden baskets are 12 to 15 inches in height, and were formerly used by Apache women for carrying wood, wild foods, and other supplies. Smaller ones were made to be given to young girls.

Since strength and durability were the qualities sought, the twined water bottles were nearly always undecorated and roughly made. Again, the material used varies from area to area. Willow, sumac (*Rhus trilobata*), and squawberry (*Vaccineum stamineum*), are the most common. Diagonal twining is nearly always used. Ground juniper leaves and red ochre are rubbed into the fabric, and the basket is then made waterproof by smearing melted piñon pitch over the entire surface. While sizes and shapes vary a great deal, nearly all water jars have a fairly wide mouth and a flaring neck.

Now that most food is purchased at a grocery store and is carried home in paper bags in the back of a pickup truck, and water can be carried and stored in a cheap plastic container, the only reason to continue making baskets is to supplement cash income. As a result, the fine close coiled baskets which often required months to weave, have almost been totally discontinued in favor of the much more quickly-made twined baskets. While the carrying baskets and water bottles are

*1.6 This contemporary Western
Apache twined water bottle (*tus) *received
a piñon gum coating on the inside only.*
DON DEDERA

still being made on both reservations, they too reflect the changing times. Some contemporary burden baskets are much coarser in weave, are generally made of rougher materials, and come in artificially large and small sizes (Fig. 1.7). The native tanned deerskin has been replaced by commercially tanned leather purchased from Tandy's and even the "tin cones" are now often aluminum and have lost much of the cheerful tinkle that used to accompany movement. The water bottle is rougher than ever. Barn red paint has, in some instances, replaced the red ochre, and even the coating of piñon pitch is often omitted (Fig. 1.6).

Nevertheless, some of the better contemporary examples are pleasing and find a ready market among collectors and decorators.

Yavapai

The Yavapai have been called by so many different names that their very identity has been obscured. While the Yavapai are members of the Yuman linguistic family, they have long been associated with the Athabaskan-speaking Apache. They adopted a good many Apache cultural traits, and even joined forces with them to raid the Hualapai, Havasupai, Maricopa, and Pima. As a result they were often referred to as the Yuma-Apache, Mohave-Apache, Yavapai-Apache, or perhaps most often, simply *Apache.*

1.7 Contemporary Western Apache carrying baskets from the San Carlos area.
DON DEDERA

1.8 (Below) A group of Western Apache baskets from the early part of this century. The basket on the left is a close-coiled storage jar. Three twined water bottles (tus) appear in the center of the grouping; their shiny appearance is caused by a coating of piñon gum. To the right are two twined carrying baskets and a close-coiled shallow bowl (only partially visible).
EDWARD S. CURTIS

The Yavapai were divided into 3 subtribes, the Northeastern, the Southeastern, and the Western Yavapai. They ranged over a territory of about 20,000 square miles (from central Arizona west to the Colorado River), yet they probably never numbered more than 1,500. They subsisted primarily by hunting and gathering, and thus were forced to migrate seasonally.

Yavapai close-coiled baskets are so similar in technique, materials, and designs to those of the Western Apache, that for the most part, no distinction was made between the work of these two tribes (again, the Apache has received all credit). This similarity is undoubtedly due, at least in part, to Yavapai confinement on the San Carlos Reservation between 1875 and 1900. However, it would be difficult to determine who influenced whom, and to what extent, during this period. The sheer numerical advantage of the Western Apache would be a strong argument in favor of that group's dominance, but baskets that are now recognized as very distinctly Yavapai in design were collected at Ft. McDowell in the first decade after the Yavapai returned there in 1900. This would suggest that the Yavapai had succeeded in maintaining at least some degree of artistic independence throughout this period, and it is conceivable that they had some influence on the basketry of the Apache. Southwestern Athabaskans are known to be great cultural borrowers.

One type of design layout that is characteristically Yavapai consists of concentric, expanding stars (commonly 5 to 7 points), which form several bands of opposing areas of light and dark, in which appear alternate positive and negative figures. Ironically, this particular design layout is perhaps the one most eagerly sought by unknowing collectors as an example of "classic" *Apache* basketry (Fig. 1.9).

Very few Yavapai baskets are being made today. There are a few experienced weavers at Ft. McDowell who are attempting to keep the tradition alive, with but marginal success. An occasional basket is also produced in both the Middle Verde and Prescott areas.

Pima

The Pimas, in native times, were referred to as the River People. They subsisted by irrigation farming and lived in permanent villages along the Gila and Salt rivers in southern Arizona. While the Pimas were basically a peaceful people, they were capable of defending themselves well when under attack. The Pima did not resist acculturation as did the neighboring Apache, but actually seemed to invite it.

During the latter half of the 19th century, the Pima were subjected to the worst influences of White civilization. The Gila River was diverted upstream for White use, and as a result the once-prosperous Pimas were reduced to poverty and starvation. By 1900 little remained of the traditional Pima culture.

It is quite possible, however, that due to this period of poverty, Pima basketry survived. Although basketry had ceased being important culturally, it now became important economically. Pima women had little opportunity for other employment, so many turned to basket making as a source of cash income.

Pima basket makers are best known for their beautifully decorated, close-coiled bowls. Most were between 12 and 24 inches in diameter and from three to eight inches in depth. The larger and deeper basket bowls were primarily used for carrying. The loaded basket was balanced on the head and carried without support from the hands (Fig. 1.10). The smaller and shallower basket bowls were used for the preparation and serving of food.

The light sewing material is normally willow, though cottonwood was sometimes used. The black material used in the designs is devil's-claw, and the foundation is a bundle of finely split cattail stems (Fig. 1.11). Occasionally a rust or pinkish tint is seen in Pima basketry designs. Both are dyes, and tend to fade badly if exposed to sunlight. The work direction is to the left.

Pima basketry designs are predominately geometric, and often very complex (Fig. 1.11a). The center of the bowl is nearly always a solid black circle which quite often plays an important part in the design. The basic patterns employed by the Pima are relatively few, but the variations on these themes seem almost endless.

In addition to these basic geometric designs, which tend to be strictly adhered to by the conservative weavers, there are designs that are originated by individual weavers. These defy description because they are as varied as the imaginations of the women who weave them. However, only a small percent of Pima baskets fall into this category.

In addition to the fine close-coiled bowls, the Pimas made several other types of baskets. Especially worthy of note is the *kiaha* or burden basket which was used by Pima and Papago women for carrying heavy loads (Fig. 1.13).

Beginning about the turn of the century, in addition to the baskets made for native use, the Pima began making baskets to sell to outsiders. A proliferation of new shapes appeared. Among the hottest-selling items were napkin rings, wastepaper baskets (Fig. 1.12), and excellent miniatures (Fig. 1.14). This era was rather short lived. Due to the ever-increasing availability of off-reservation agricultural work, which was more lucrative, most of the younger women were lured away from basketry and into farm labor.

Today there are very few Pima weavers. Most of them live on the Gila River Reservation, but an occasional basket is produced at Salt River as well. Overall, the quality of the work has remained amazingly high, and traditional forms still predominate.

1.12 (Left) Footed deep baskets, such as this one, represent a commercial adaptation expressly for sale to non-Indians.
JERRY JACKA
Heard Museum Collection

1.13 The kiaha, *or carrying basket, was made by both the Pima and Papago.*
JERRY JACKA

1.14 (Below) Pima weavers also excelled in the production of fine miniatures.
JERRY JACKA
Heard Museum Collection

Papago

The Papago, who live in extreme southern Arizona, are basically the same people as the Pima. The cultural differences between the two tribes are largely the result of adaptation to environmental differences. Since the Papago area was without rivers or permanent streams, these people were unable to farm as intensively as the Pima. They were forced to rely more upon hunting and gathering, and had to move about seasonally in search of water.

Traditionally, Papago close-coiled basketry was very similar to that of the Pima. While there are some characteristics that are more often associated with the Papago, there is perhaps as much variation in materials, technique, and design within the Papago area, as there is between the Papago and Pima groups as a whole. Papago baskets are more apt to have thicker walls, broader bases, larger masses of dark in the design, and bear grass foundations. Pima baskets tend to have thinner walls, are more flexible, have more active and complex designs, and show superior craftsmanship. Some thick-walled Papago bowls are so tightly woven they are watertight. Plaited basketry was made in earlier years by both Papago and Pima weavers.

Sometime around 1900 the Papago began to substitute yucca for willow, which was much more scarce and had to be acquired by trade. Yucca, however, was used only in those baskets intended for sale to outsiders, and willow baskets were still made for native use (Fig. 1.15). This use of yucca marked the beginning of what was to become the almost complete commercialization of Papago basketry. Soon new forms, new designs, and quicker weaving techniques appeared. All of these changes proved to be extremely popular with the non-Indian buyers whose main interest was the acquisition of an inexpensive souvenir.

At the present time Papago weavers number in the hundreds and produce most of the Indian baskets seen in the trading posts and curio shops in the Southwest. While much of this work is quite coarse and rather hastily made, a few superior weavers are contributing a limited quantity of high-quality basketry.

The split stitch weaves seem to be the most popular at present.
The white yucca stitches are widely spaced, leaving much of the pale
green bear grass foundation exposed. Subtle patterns can be created by
careful placement of the stitches (Fig. 1.16).

Closely-stitched coiled baskets of sun-bleached white yucca
with designs executed in one or more colors are also made. Baskets of
this type are the high point of modern Papago weaving. Devil's-claw
provides the black; green and yellow are obtained from the narrow-leafed
yucca. The root of the same plant provides a dark red-brown which is
occasionally used. After the completion of each coil, the weaver pounds
it flat with a hammer or smooth stone. This produces the almost flat
walls found in the modern Papago baskets (Fig. 1.17).

Contemporary Papago baskets are made in a great variety
of sizes and shapes. The only limiting factors seem to be the degree of
a weaver's inventiveness and perseverance, and the thickness of the pur-
chaser's wallet. Large simple geometric designs predominate, but life
forms are also common.

Miniature baskets constructed of horsehair have been made
for some time. While these come in a large assortment of forms, human
and animal effigies have been especially popular with collectors. In the
last few years monofilament fishing line or nylon thread is sometimes
substituted for horsehair.

Baskets constructed of baling wire, color-coded telephone
wire, and other types of wire are a fairly recent Papago development.
The technique is similar to that used in the *kiaha,* and the only tools
needed are pliers and a hammer.

19

Hopi

The Hopis are the only Southwestern Indian tribe that produces better coiled basketry today than it did 100 years ago. This is largely due to the fact that the Hopi have clung tenaciously to their native culture, and basketry has retained at least a portion of its former importance to these people. Quantities of baskets are still needed for gifts at Hopi weddings, and for ceremonial purposes.

Each of the three Hopi mesas has its own artistic specialty. First Mesa produces pottery, Second Mesa provides close-coiled basketry, and Third Mesa furnishes wicker basketry.

Second Mesa baskets are made of finely split yucca sewn around a grass-bundle foundation (*Hilaria jamesii*). Baskets made during the second half of the 19th century were constructed of very thick coils (often 1-inch diameter), and tended to have simple, all-over designs. Aniline dyes were introduced during the 1880's with less-than-favorable results. However, as the result of a revival which began in the early years of this century, a very successful return to native dyes has been made. Plaques, shallow bowls, and deep bowls are the common forms, but other shapes also appear (Fig. 1.18). The work direction is to the left.

1.18 (Opposite page and below center and right)
Contemporary coiled plaques from Second Mesa.
RAY MANLEY

1.19 (Left and lower left) Third Mesa wicker
basketry is the most colorful native basketry
in the Southwest.
JERRY JACKA
Heard Museum Collection

Modern Hopi baskets have much smaller coils and the designs are more complex. The use of color (commonly black, red, yellow, and green on a white background) is also more complex in later work. The black and red are native dyes while the others are natural colors obtained from the yucca. Common motifs are kachina masks, full kachinas, deer, eagles, corn, butterflies, clouds, rainbows, highly conventionalized life forms, and geometric arrangements.

Third Mesa weavers excel in the wicker technique, which is the simplest variation of twining (Fig. 1.19). In wicker only one weft is used at a time, instead of two as in plain twining. Sumac or wild currant is used for the framework (warp) and peeled stems of the rabbit brush are used for the weft. This is the most brilliantly colored of all Southwestern basketry. While commercial dyes were extensively used around the turn of the century, native vegetal and mineral dyes have been favored since that time. Mineral dyes are rubbed or painted on. When vegetal dyes are used, the prepared stems are first boiled in the dye, and the color is set by exposing the still-wet stems to the smoke of raw burning wool.

Plaques and bowls are the dominant forms. A noticeable hump, caused by the crossing of the warp bundles, appears in the center of the bottom of these baskets. Designs occur in great variety, including static bands, whirls, life forms, and kachinas.

Several other utilitarian forms are made on all three mesas. The plaited "ring basket," or sifter has been described. Plaited and wicker piki trays are still made and used, but the wicker peach basket (carrying basket), which was made and used by Hopi men, has not survived.

Havasupai

The Havasupai (people of the blue-green waters) are a very small tribe residing in Havasu Canyon, a tributary of the Grand Canyon. They are primarily subsistence farmers, irrigating small fields of corn, beans, and squash with water diverted from Havasu Creek. In former times, they spent the winter months atop the plateau where they hunted and gathered piñon nuts and other wild foods, but returned to the canyon floor in the spring to plant.

In technique, materials, and design, Havasupai close-coiled baskets much resemble those of the Apache and Yavapai. Older Havasupai coiled baskets often had braided rims and bright aniline colors. The black rim, which is almost universal on Apache and Yavapai baskets, is often absent on Havasupai ware. Thus, Havasupai baskets frequently have the appearance of being unfinished Yavapai or Apache baskets.

The peak in Havasupai basketry occurred in the 1930's. Better preparation of materials, a broadened range of forms, and an expanded awareness of design characterized this period. The best work of this period rivals the best done anywhere in the Southwest (Fig. 1.20).

The Havasupai also make several types of baskets in the twining technique. Large conical burden baskets, piñon-pitch-covered water jars, and shallow trays are the most common forms. Both plain and diagonal twining are used. Although catclaw (*Acacia gregii*) is the preferred twining material, several other plants are used as well. Simple banded designs in devil's-claw are the usual decoration (Fig. 1.20).

At present, a number of Havasupai women are producing baskets of various types. While most are small and somewhat hastily made for sale to the ever-increasing number of tourists, a few weavers are doing exceptional work.

1.20a During the 1930s, Havasupai weavers produced some of the finest coiled basketry known in the Southwest.
JERRY JACKA

1.20b Havasupai basket weaver at work.
R. H. PEEBLES

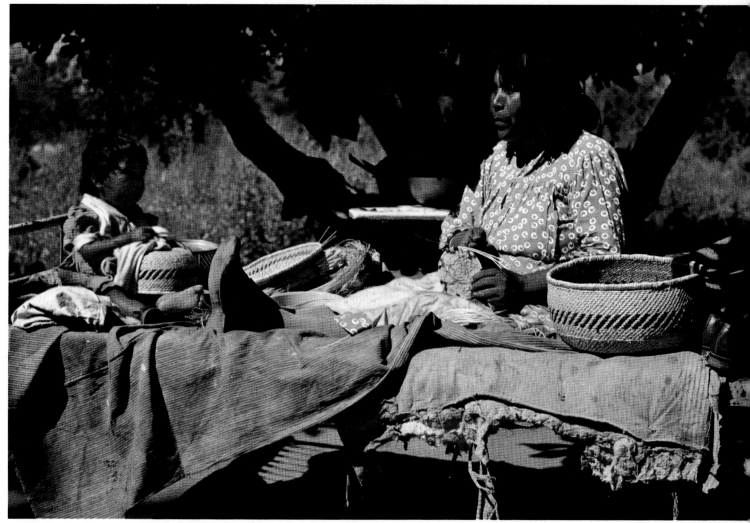

Chemehuevi

The Chemehuevi, technically an offshoot of the Southern Paiute, were adopted into the Southwest by the Mohave. Prior to about the middle of the 19th century, they roamed over the eastern half of the Mohave Desert in California subsisting by hunting and gathering. At the allowance of the Mohave, they began drifting over to the Colorado River where they began floodwater farming in the Chemehuevi Valley and Colorado Valley. Chemehuevi religious concepts, warfare, and mode of subsistence were heavily influenced by the Mohave.

While the Chemehuevi were eventually given their own reservation in Chemehuevi Valley, they now reside primarily on the Colorado River Indian Reservation near Parker, Arizona.

Chemehuevi coiled basketry is noted for simplicity of design and perfection of technique (Fig. 1.21). The three-rod triangular foundation is used, but the work direction is to the right. The latter trait is unique in the Southwest, as all other tribes (except their left-handed members) coil to the left. Willow, and occasionally cottonwood, is used as the principal sewing material while designs are executed in devil's-claw, juncus, or, rarely, split flicker quill.

Chemehuevi baskets made before 1900 have extremely simple geometric designs in black with large undecorated areas (Fig. 1.23). Much of their beauty lies in the almost perfect control of contour and fine even stitching. Rather small jars with gracefully rounded shoulders and shallow bowls are the most common forms. Some aniline dyes were used in the late 1800's, but soon went out of fashion.

Later Chemehuevi work featured more complex designs, often in three or four natural colors, and life forms were introduced. Birds, butterflies, snakes, lizards, bugs, and plants became fairly common (Fig. 1.22). Anthropomorphic motifs were never as popular with the Chemehuevi as they were with the Apache, Yavapai, and Havasupai.

25

Very few baskets have been made in recent years, although there have been some attempts to create a revival. Twined basketry is no longer made by the Chemehuevi.

Other Tribes

A number of other Southwest tribes also make, or have made, basketry. The Navajo formerly made fairly good close-coiled baskets on a two-rod-and-bundle foundation. Little basketry is made by the Navajo at present, and even the baskets used in Navajo ceremonies are most often made to Navajo specifications by the Utes or Paiutes. The Hualapai in the past did about the same range of basketry as the Havasupai, but with some variation in weaving material, and a strong preference for aniline dye. Today, small diagonally-twined bowls with geometric bands in bright aniline dye colors are made for sale to tourists.

Two Apache groups in New Mexico also produce a limited amount of basketry. The northern tribe, the Jicarilla, weave rather coarsely coiled deep bowls and straight sided baskets with lids. Recent work is decorated with simple to fairly complex geometric designs, life forms, and floral motifs — all in often garish aniline dye colors. The principal sewing material is sumac. The foundation is either three or five rods bunched. The Mescalero, who live in southern New Mexico, make large shallow bowls with massive geometric designs in soft natural colors. Three types of foundation are used: two rods and a bundle, three rods and a bundle, or a wood slat and a bundle. All are arranged in a vertical position that results in a wide and flexible coil. The sewing material is yucca which, by different degrees of bleaching, gives green, yellow, and white; red-brown is obtained from the root of the narrow-leafed yucca.

The Rio Grande Pueblos have lost most of their basketry tradition. Plaited "ring baskets" are made at Jemez, and some coarse wicker work is occasionally done at Santo Domingo and a few of the other pueblos. The Puebloans still have a great fondness for fine examples of coiled basketry, and much of it is still to be seen in their homes; practically all of it, however, has been acquired by trading with other tribes who continue to produce basketry.

The fact that native forms of basketry have survived to the present, even in limited quantity, is a testimonal to the tenacity with which the Southwestern Indians have clung to their native cultures.

*1.22 Maggie Painter, Chemehuevi from the
Colorado River Reservation near Parker,
Arizona, is best remembered for her
"butterfly" design, although she created
other zoomorphic patterns including the
shallow "rattlesnake" basket pictured below.
Circa 1960.*
JERRY JACKA

Economics alone cannot explain its continued existence (economically, basketry has not been viable for generations). Even at the crest of the present wave of popularity enjoyed by all things Indian, few full-time basket weavers can earn more than two thousand dollars per year, while top people in other areas of Indian art have achieved incomes approaching those of corporate executives.

Once-plentiful weaving materials have fallen victim to progress, and have been sacrificed in the names of "phreatophyte eradication," "channelization," "watershed management," and other programs said to be in the public interest. Reservation water tables have fallen; rivers and streams have disappeared.

Individual basket weavers have not received the attention or developed prestigious names like those associated with Indian artists in the other major arts and crafts categories. One reason for this is that the best basket weavers are, quite often, strongholds of Indian conservatism. In many of the traditional Indian cultures of the Southwest, while excellence is perfectly acceptable (or even expected), it is considered

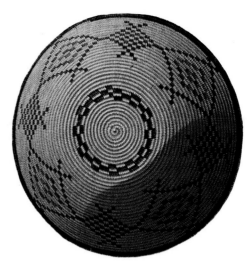

improper to boast or become vain about one's own accomplishments. A second, and more practical reason is that a basket weaver's production is limited to only a few major works per year. Especially large or fine examples can require a full year or more to complete. As a result, there is an insufficient quantity of work to allow a significantly wide distribution to attract even a regional following. For example, to stage a one-person showing of about twenty major works by a single weaver, five to ten years of production time would be required. Unfortunately, in the meantime the artist would be receiving no recognition or income. If the show was a sellout, and other galleries wanted similar showings, it would require an additional five to ten years to fill each request — providing that no commissions from individuals were accepted in the interim. It should be obvious that such an arrangement would probably not be looked upon with much enthusiasm by either the artist or the gallery.

While a few commercially adapted forms will probably linger on for some time, at the present time there seems little doubt that basketry, as a native Southwestern art form, has nearly fulfilled its destiny.

29

2/Weaving

by Joe Ben Wheat, Ph.D.

When Coronado and the Spanish conquistadores "discovered" the Southwest in 1540, they were surprised and pleased to find the village-dwelling Indians they called Pueblos wearing cotton clothing of their own manufacture. The main garment was a small blanket woven wider than long and decorated by dyeing, painting, or sometimes by embroidery, folded under one arm, fastened over the other shoulder, and held in place by a woven sash. These blankets, or *mantas,* served as dresses for the women. In cold weather both women and men wore them as shawls.

These early blankets were woven on a wide, upright loom developed by the Pueblo Indians about A.D. 800. Most of them were of plain weave in which both foundation warp and the moving weft were visible, and in diagonal or diamond twill weave; but a few were woven in tapestry technique in which the warps were concealed by the weft.

In 1540, Coronado's men drove herds of sheep and goats along with them, to serve only as food. In 1598, the Spanish colonists brought sheep and goats to supply not only meat but also wool for their own looms. The sheep introduced by the Spanish was the country sheep of southern Spain—the *churro.* In a land of little water and with only hand tools to prepare and spin the wool, the long, straight, almost greaseless fleece of the churro was ideal.

It was not long until the Puebloans, taught by the missionaries, learned to spin and weave wool as they had previously done with cotton. The churro came in creamy white, and in golden tan to dark brown-black — natural colors that mark the early blankets of the Southwest.

The Spanish brought the blue dye, indigo, and later other dyes such as logwood, brazilwood, and the insect cochineal, but they also took over some of the native vegetal dyes of the Pueblos. The short, wide, Pueblo manta now began to appear with dark wool center and indigo blue ends. It survives as the Pueblo woman's ceremonial dress of today. Other pieces were decorated in alternating horizontal stripes of brown and white, with occasional touches of blue.

Along with the sheep, the Spanish brought their own loom (or rather, the knowledge of how to make and use it). They introduced a homemade version of the European horizontal treadle loom on which they wove piece goods and blankets or sarapes. In contrast to the Pueblo

2.1 The combination of vibrant aniline and earthy vegetal dyes makes a striking tapestry. Woven by Philomena Yazzie, it is in the Richard A. Voit Collection.
FREDERICK T. SHARP

manta, the Spanish sarape was woven in two pieces, each about two feet wide and seven feet long, sewn together to make a long, narrow blanket. These are known as Old Rio Grande blankets. Most of their weaving was in tapestry technique, by which complicated designs could be introduced by changing the weft colors wherever desired, as in the famous tapestries of Europe. However, the earliest Spanish blankets probably were decorated only by stripes of blue, brown, and white. One of the favorite Old Rio Grande blanket patterns consisted of zones of alternating stripes of natural brown and indigo blue, separated by bands of white. This style of decoration, called the Moki pattern, was taken over by the Pueblos and by the Navajo, who called it the "Mexican Pelt."

The Navajo and their Apache kinsmen were relative latecomers to the Southwest, arriving before the Spanish but long after the Pueblos. They were first called *Apaches de Navajú,* or Apaches of the great fields. When they first came into view, they were mentioned as farmers and raiders, and were noted for the quality and beauty of their fine baskets, but they did not weave cloth. Their homeland was northwest of Santa Fe, but by 1650 they were trading and raiding far beyond their borders. They appear to have been increasing in numbers and strength, and Pueblo Indians taken in their raids were incorporated into the tribe. It seems likely that the Navajo learned to weave from

2.2 (Left) Phase 3 Chief Blanket with terraced diamond center, corner quarter-diamonds, and half-diamonds at ends and sides. Chief Blankets were very popular and were traded widely to other Indians.
JOE BEN WHEAT

2.3 This Chief Blanket has crosses rather than diamonds. Three-ply saxony yarn was used in this blanket.
ARIZONA PHOTOGRAPHIC ASSOCIATES

some of these captured Puebloans, for they clearly took over the Pueblo upright loom and mastered the Pueblo weaving techniques. We do not know precisely when this occurred. It may well have been before the Pueblos revolted against the Spanish in 1680 and drove them from the upper Rio Grande Valley. When the Spanish returned in 1692, many Puebloans fled to the Navajo country, and some believe that the Navajo learned to weave at that time. By 1706 the Navajo were weaving blankets and cloth, and trading them to Puebloans and Spaniards alike, at trade fairs held in their own country.

Since the Navajo took over the Pueblo vertical loom and methods of preparing and spinning wool, it is not surprising that they wove many Pueblo-like garments. One of these was the wide, short, one-piece, woman's manta dress with dark wool center and blue, diamond twill ends; which, except for technical details such as the selvage edges, corner closures, and frequent appearance of "lazy lines," are typically Puebloan.

Pueblo weavers usually carry the weft completely across the growing blanket, but the Navajo woman usually weaves her blanket a section at a time, leaving diagonal lines where these sections are later joined. These are called lazy lines.

33

Another short, wide fabric eventually developed into the so-called Chief Blanket. The earliest ones had wide alternating stripes of brown-black and white. By 1800, the end and center stripes of black had been widened, and narrow stripes of blue were added. These are known as First Phase blankets. Later, during the Second Phase, rectangles of red were introduced into the blue stripes. Ultimately, Third Phase developed, in which the color blocks became enlarged into nine decorative "spots," usually a full diamond at the center, quarter-diamonds at each corner, and half-diamonds at the center of the ends and sides (Fig. 2.2). Although this is considered to be standard, many design variations were woven by the Navajo (Fig. 2.3).

By the late 1700's, the Pueblo-like manta dress gave way to a two-piece dress made of identical small blankets with dark centers and decorative end panels, at first in blue, and, by 1785, with blue designs on a red ground (Fig. 2.4). The Navajo did not have a good red dye, but the Spanish imported a fine crimson cloth, called *bayeta,* from England. The Navajo soon learned to ravel this cloth and re-weave the red threads along with their own fine-spun yarns. The two-piece dress was in use until nearly 1900. One other garment, a one-piece shawl, or manta, with designs like those on the dresses, was woven in the Puebloan shape until it was replaced by the commercially-manufactured "Pendleton" robes or shawls in the late 1800's.

From the Spanish, the Navajo quickly adopted the long blanket, or sarape, with its emphasis on tapestry weave; and it is in the sarape that Navajo weaving reached its highest pinnacle. The earliest blankets were dominated by stripes — simple stripes, compound stripes, and complex, figured stripes, used singly or in rhythmic clusters. Stripes continue even today, but the creative genius of the Navajo woman was not satisfied by stripes. In her coiled baskets, she had woven bands edged by triangles with stepped or terraced outlines. By manipulating the weft properly, stepped-edge triangles could be woven in tapestry, to make bands across the blanket. If the triangles were opposed point to point, they enclosed negative diamond-shaped figures; but if they were opposed with the points offset, they formed a negative zigzag figure between them. This relationship of positive to negative design units, combined with variation of color of the different design elements and the background, produced bold and complex patterns that dominated Navajo

2.4 Two-piece dresses were in favor from 1785 to about 1890. The crimson panels are woven from threads raveled from fine bayeta *cloth. Early dress with open terraced diamonds.*
ARIZONA PHOTOGRAPHIC ASSOCIATES
Read Mullan Collection

weaving from 1800 to about 1870 (Fig. 2.5). These Classic blankets usually had a ground of raveled crimson cloth, with designs in white and dark blue. Native yellow or green was used in small amounts. Many were woven so tightly that they held water.

In 1821, Mexico won her independence from Spain, and opened her New Mexico border to American traders across the Santa Fe Trail. More red cloth for raveling came in, much of it manufactured in New England mills; and a fine, silky, three-ply commercial yarn, called Saxony, was introduced in 1822. In 1846, the United States "conquered" New Mexico, and the intermittent warfare and slavery that had persisted since the 1600's between Navajo and Spanish, now became an American problem. In 1863, the Americans, under Kit Carson, defeated the Navajo by destroying their homes, crops, and sheep, and exiled them to Bosque Redondo in eastern New Mexico. This was a turning point in Navajo relationships and in Navajo weaving. For four long years the Navajo suffered in isolation in an alien world. They had few sheep left to supply their weaving needs, so Army-supplied blankets and many kinds of trade cloth, much of it dyed with the newly-invented aniline dyes, were raveled

2.5 Navajo Classic Sarape of about 1840. The bold, simple design uses variations of terraced triangles making zigzags and diamonds. It is woven in indigo blue and natural white on a crimson bayeta *ground.*
JOE BEN WHEAT

to supplement wool from their own sheep. Aniline-dyed three-ply yarns began to replace the older Saxony yarns and were combined with the home-spun and raveled yarns in weaving. Although some blankets of striking beauty were woven during this time, the bold designs of Classic times tended to become smaller and stereotyped. Usually they were set into wide stripes or panels on a plain ground. New design elements, such as the meander and crosses, were introduced. Weaving was less carefully done (Fig. 2.7), and more and more pieces were made for sale to the Navajos' American captors.

In order to understand the next development in Navajo weaving, we must turn back to about 1800. Southwestern weaving has always had a strong commercial element. In the 1600's, Spanish cloth was sold into northern Mexico. The early 1700's saw the Navajo selling blankets to both Spaniards and Puebloans, and in 1776, the Hopis were selling blankets to the Indians along the Gila River in Arizona. By 1800, Spanish weaving had greatly degenerated and Navajo weaving was the most important commercial product of New Mexico, being sold in the annual trade fairs of northern Mexico. In 1807, the local government made a contract with Spanish master-weaver Don Ricardo Bazan and his brother, to come to Santa Fe and instruct the Spanish in improved methods of spinning, dyeing, and weaving.

Shortly after this, a number of changes began to appear in Old Rio Grande weaving, the most important being the appearance of the design layout system and decorative elements used by the sarape makers of Saltillo and San Miguel in Mexico. In its classic form, this style featured a bold central motif, usually of concentric diamonds with serrate edges embellished by minute figures. This central figure was set on a background of intricate, vertically oriented, zigzag stripes, surrounded by a complex figured border. Because the Old Rio Grande weavers could not match the fine wools, dyes, and loom-work, the result was a simplified and coarsened version of these fine Mexican sarapes. Many of these were woven during the middle 1800's. In 1867, four thousand Old Rio Grande sarapes were issued to the Navajo at Bosque Redondo, bringing the Navajo, for the first time, into close contact with the Mexican design system filtered once through their Spanish weavers.

When the Navajo returned to their old homeland in 1868, they were a people in transition. They took with them new materials, new designs, and new customers. The new Saltillo, or Mexican, design system was rarely copied exactly. Rather, the concentric serrate diamonds were taken apart and rearranged to make horizontal zigzag stripes with serrate rather than terraced edges, or several small serrate figures might be woven side by side to make a decorative panel across the blanket. Frequently, they combined terraced and serrate units in the same fabric, and even wove concentric diamonds with terraced edges (Fig. 2.6). By 1885, serrate motifs and elements became the dominant pattern in Navajo weaving. Many of these figures were arranged vertically, and borders became more and more common.

From 1870 on, Anglo-American clothing and blankets rapidly replaced the garments that the Navajo had woven for themselves; but the Navajo continued to sell their blankets to the Puebloans and increasingly to the American soldiers and traders moving into the area. The soldiers bought them as souvenirs of their Western experience. The traders bought them to sell to the tourists who had begun to visit the great Southwest, and to the settlers who had begun to live there. After the railroads came, in the early 1880's, the trickle of visitors became a flood, and the demand for Navajo weaving grew.

New designs and developments came rapidly. The two-face blanket, with a different design on each side, was invented. Pictorial

2.6 (Left) Transitional Period Child's Blanket of about 1870, with hand-spun, and 3-ply aniline-dyed early Germantown yarns. Zigzag stripes with serrate edges make rows of small diamonds across the blanket, combined with small vertical "lightning" figures and conventional terraced-edge open diamonds.
JOE BEN WHEAT

2.7 (Below) Late Classic Child's Blanket, woven about 1865, of hand-spun, raveled cloth, and 3-ply saxony yarn. Meanders and simple stripes replace the bold terraced designs of earlier times.
JOE BEN WHEAT

2.8 (Right) Wedge-weave blanket with handspun wool dyed with Rio Grande Valley Spanish vegetal dyes. This blanket was woven about 1870 by a Navajo woman slave in a Spanish household in the San Luis Valley of Colorado, using the pastel dyes of the Old Rio Grande weavers.
JOE BEN WHEAT

blankets became very popular as the women, freed from some of their former constraints, wove into their blankets anything that struck their fancy — box labels, cattle, sheep, horses, railroad trains, and flying birds. The wedge-weave tapestry, with stripes woven diagonally across the warps rather than straight across, was invented (Fig. 2.8), and there appeared a sudden flood of twilled saddle blankets to go under their saddles, and small, fancy saddle throws to go on top of them, where only sheepskins had been used before. They even wove an imitation sheepskin in the tufted weave. Aniline dyes more and more replaced the earlier natural dyes.

About 1875, four-ply aniline-dyed "Germantown" yarns, named after the Germantown, Pennsylvania, mills, began to replace the earlier three-ply aniline yarns (Fig. 2.11). The fineness of these yarns and the multiplicity of colors soon led to the weaving of the intricately patterned, highly colored "eye dazzlers" of the 1890's.

In part, the Navajo used these machine-spun yarns and their coarse, raveled, counterparts because their flocks were still small. When the Navajo returned to their homeland, the government supplied them with sheep purchased in the Rio Grande Valley. These sheep were a cross between the old Spanish churro and the newly-introduced merino,

39

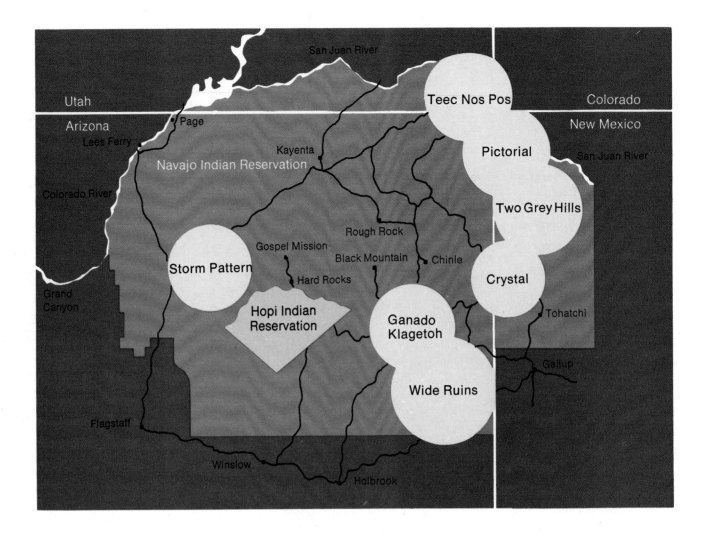

and while they produced fine mutton, their wool was short, very fine and kinky, and heavy with grease, characteristics which made it difficult to clean and spin. The kinky, greasy wool from these "improved" sheep did not take aniline dyes well. The inevitable result was a degeneration of Navajo weaving which, for a while, threatened to destroy the art.

It was at this point that the traders began to develop a market for these coarse blankets, for use as rugs. It was not long until the weavers in certain areas began to specialize in designs and colors. Sometimes these were prompted by the traders, but some were based on the preferences of the weavers of an area. Before this time, the basic patterns were used by most weavers across the Reservation (Fig. 2.9).

The first of the regional developments began around Ganado, Arizona. About 1890, Don Lorenzo Hubbell began to work with the Ganado weavers to improve the quality of their weaving. Aniline dyes, except for the strong "Ganado Red," were discouraged. Natural wool in white and black, and these carded together to make shades of gray, were encouraged. Paintings were made of good, old designs; and new designs, with central motifs surrounded by borders, were introduced. One of the old designs was the Moki pattern, often woven with Germantown yarn (Fig. 2.10). Customers could select design, color, and size. Room-sized and larger rugs became a specialty (Fig. 2.13). About 1900, Hubbell contracted to supply many of his better rugs to Fred Harvey, for his Indian shops, so gradually there began an improvement in Navajo rugs.

40

2.9 (Left) Principal weaving districts on the Navajo reservation. Storm patterns are usually distinguished by zigzag lines, lightning, and storm-related symbols. Ganado rugs are noted for their brilliant dark red character. Wide Ruin is the prime vegetal dye center of the reservation. Crystal rugs are the most uncomplicated of contemporary designs. Two Grey Hills are often the tightest woven, most expensive rugs from all sections. Pictorial rugs are noted for their Yeibechai figures. The Teec Nos area produces rugs of the most complex patterns, often with a strong outline design.

2.10 (Right) A "Moki Pattern" blanket woven of Germantown yarns with typical Navajo overlay pattern. The Moki Pattern was a specialty of Hubbell's Ganado weavers.
PETER BLOOMER

2.11 (Below) Germantown Blanket. Fine-spun yarn and brilliant colors are blended in an innovative design featuring both terraced and serrate-outline figures. Heavy, sewn-on fringes were frequently added to make Germantown blankets and rugs more elaborate.
PETER BLOOMER

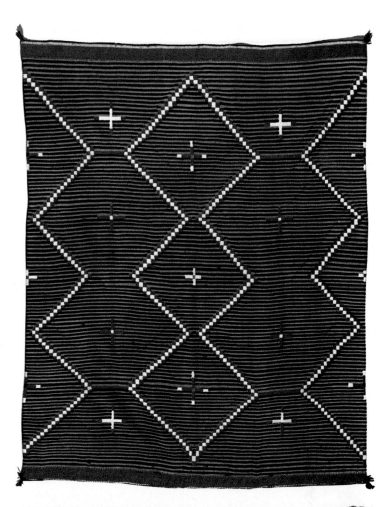

2.12 *J. B. Moore Crystal copy of a late Classic blanket using terraced diamonds and zigzags with small dashes inspired by Mexican blanketry. All hand-spun, with white, red, and black rather than indigo blue. This pattern is shown in Moore's 1903 catalogue.*
ARIZONA PHOTOGRAPHIC ASSOCIATES
Harmsen's Western Americana Collection

2.13 *(Below) The second largest Navajo rug ever woven, this measures 31 feet long and 19 feet wide. It took Minnie Many-horses 23 months to weave it, with 23 helpers. It is more complex than most Ganado rugs but makes use of typical layout and pattern.*
JOE BEN WHEAT

2.14 *(Right) Crystal rug with Oriental motif, from* Indian Blankets and Their Makers.

Another trader instrumental in reviving the ailing craft was J. B. Moore, who bought the trading post at Crystal, New Mexico, in 1896. Like Hubbell, he first made copies of earlier blankets (Fig. 2.12). Also like Hubbell, he encouraged the use of natural wool colors, the limited use of better-quality aniline dyes, better designing, and better workmanship. For his quality rugs, he sent wool back East to be properly cleaned. Then the wool was spun by his best spinners. The yarns were dyed by his wife, and then distributed to his best weavers to be made into rugs. Between 1903 and 1911 he distributed catalogues and flyers with color plates showing a series of patterns that could be ordered by mail. Pattern, color scheme, size, and quality could be ordered by the customer. Some of Moore's designs were simplified copies of Oriental rugs from Turkey (Fig. 2.14); others combined old Navajo elements with elements from various sources. Many of these rugs featured not one, but two, or even more, borders which were apt to contain complex figures of their own (Fig. 2.15). In 1911, Moore published the "Storm" pattern, which is still woven today, particularly by the Western Navajo (Fig. 2.16). Still other elements, especially layout, influenced development of other regional styles, such as those at Teec Nos Pos and Two Grey Hills.

Two Grey Hills, and its neighbor trading post, Toadlena, are just across the Chuska Mountains and a bit north from Crystal. For many years, the Navajo in this area had been weaving rugs of routine

quality, in geometric patterns, but differing from most others in that their makers showed a decided preference for using only the natural-color wools — gray, white, black, and brown. The Two Grey Hills weavers did not share the common Navajo liking for red. About 1915, things began to change through the efforts of Ed Davies and George Bloomfield, who then owned the two trading posts. They set out to improve local rugs.

The success of J. B. Moore's Crystal rugs probably served as a stimulus, for most of the early Two Grey Hills rugs show the same basic patterns. These feature a complex central motif surrounded by borders. Every corner of the rug had some motif woven into it. According to Bloomfield's son-in-law, Charles Herring, Davies and Bloomfield gathered potsherds from the Pueblo ruins in the vicinity and worked up some rug patterns from the ancient pottery designs to add variety to the patterns already in use. Photographs were taken of the better rugs and were shown to other weavers. Bloomfield and Davies spent hours going over the rugs as they were brought in by the weavers, and made suggestions on carding the different wools together to make shades of tan and gray. By 1925, a distinctive pattern had emerged which, while resembling the Crystal rugs in some respects, was far more intricate in the development of its design (Fig. 2.17a-e).

Usually, the Two Grey Hills fabrics have a central stepped-edge diamond motif embellished with stepped or serrate frets and triangular corner elements. A complex inner border is surrounded by a plain, dark frame. Often there is a so-called spirit line that leads from the interior design panel, through the borders, to the outer edge of the

2.15 (Left) Crystal rug with complex border design and bold terraced designs (1911). From Indian Blankets and Their Makers.

2.16 "Storm" Pattern Rug from Tuba City, an almost exact copy of the first "Storm" Pattern published by J. B. Moore in 1911.
ARIZONA PHOTOGRAPHIC ASSOCIATES
Read Mullan Collection

blanket. By 1940, wall tapestries — they could no longer be called rugs — with thread-counts of 16 warps and 60 wefts to the inch, had been achieved. A few years later, Daisy Tauglechee, of Toadlena, had produced a tapestry of 24 warps and 126 wefts per inch. Today, a number of weavers produce equally fine tapestries, featuring as many as 15 shades of natural color wools, including their carded intermediate tans and grays (Fig. 2.18). Only the black wool is dyed, so that it does not fade to the reddish brown tinge of the natural black sheep wool. Pound-for-pound — today, one can say ounce-for-ounce — the Two Grey Hills tapestries are probably the most costly textiles in the world.

Teec Nos Pos Trading Post lies very near the Four Corners, where Utah, Colorado, Arizona, and New Mexico come together. One of the designs that the Navajo developed after their return from Bosque Redondo consisted of covering the entire blanket with concentric serrate diamonds built up of small triangles of different colors. Often, these blankets or rugs also had a figured border. Most were made of Germantown yarns, and in many, each triangle was outlined in still another color. As Germantown yarns went out of fashion in the early 1900's, so did the serrate-outline blanket or rug, except among the weavers in the vicinity of Teec Nos Pos. At that time, there were some very fine weavers in the area who continued to weave serrate-outline rugs, using hand-spun yarns, coloring them with aniline dyes. Such rugs are still woven today, although many weavers have returned to the use of four-ply commercial yarns. Some time after the Crystal ideas began to spread northward to other areas, the Teec Nos Pos weavers selected some of the basic ideas,

45

*2.17a (Right) The first of these five
Two Grey Hills rugs is by Julia Jumbo,
from the Richard A. Voit Collection.*
FREDERICK T. SHARP

*2.17b (Below) Grand Prize winner, 1954
Gallup Inter-tribal Indian Ceremonials,
woven by Daisy Tauglechee.*
ARIZONA PHOTOGRAPHIC ASSOCIATES

2.17c (Top) By Mildred Natoni, from the Ray Gwilliam Collection.
ARIZONA PHOTOGRAPHIC ASSOCIATES

2.17d (Bottom Left) By Elizabeth Mute, from the Richard Spivey Collection. These tapestries are in the traditional color range of Two Grey Hills.
ROBERT NUGENT

2.17e (Bottom Right) By Mary Joe Gould, from the Richard A. Voit Collection.
FREDERICK T. SHARP

such as the complex, figured borders (sometimes two or three borders), and center-dominant or paneled designs, but they continued to outline them with contrasting colors, as they had done with the serrate figures which preceded them (Fig. 2.19). In some respects, these resemble Two Grey Hills designs, but they are generally less intricate, and many now combine the use of hand-spun, aniline, and vegetal-dyed yarns with natural color wools, as well as commercial yarns (Fig. 2.20a-c).

Navajo sand paintings are religious altars, made by medicine men for use in healing ceremonies. By tradition, they must be destroyed the same day they are made, following the ceremony. Thus, their preservation in permanent form, such as in weaving, is frowned upon by the Navajo themselves. Nevertheless, more or less accurate copies of sand paintings have been woven since the turn of the century. At least two were woven in Chaco Canyon before 1900, and one near Two Grey Hills in 1904, but these have disappeared and we do not know what they looked like. By 1915, a few weavers in the Ganado area were making sand-painting rugs. Except for the early Two Grey Hills piece, which was woven by a medicine man and which created a tremendous furor among the local Navajos, the essential accuracy of these early sand-painting tapestries may be questioned. The weavers apparently felt that if some part of the sand painting was omitted or rendered incorrectly, it lessened the chances of their being struck blind for weaving them.

About 1920, at the behest of Mary Cabot Wheelwright and Franc Newcomb, the noted medicine man Hosteen Klah (Lefthanded), who lived in the Two Grey Hills area, held the proper ceremonies and began to weave his series of about 25 large, accurate, sand-painting tapestries (Fig. 2.21). Again, there was a furor, but since Klah was a powerful medicine man, these gradually came to be accepted. Klah held ceremonies for two of his nieces, and they, too, began to weave these tapestries. By 1925, some of the weavers around Lukachukai Trading Post were producing sand paintings, as well as Yei rugs (Fig. 2.22). By 1930, the Ganado weavers were again producing sand-painting tapestries. Today, most sand-painting tapestries are woven in the Two Grey Hills and Shiprock areas (Fig. 2.23). Even if they are not ceremonial rugs, they are, for the most part, beautifully woven tapestries and should be regarded as such.

Yeis are gods or spirits in the Navajo pantheon. Normally, they are depicted in the sand painting altars used in curing ceremonies, and are represented by masks worn by dancers in the Yeibechai dances. It is not known when they were first woven in textiles, but one blanket woven about 1885 has a single, small, geometric figure which terminates in a Yei mask all but lost in the welter of other figures. One of the first rugs featuring a Yei as its principal design was woven near Farmington, about 1910, by the Navajo wife of a white trader (Fig. 2.25).

49

*2.20a (Left) By Alice Nelson, from Russell Foutz
Indian Room.*
RAY MANLEY

*2.20b (Lower Left) By Emma Yabeney, from the Read
Mullan Collection.*
ARIZONA PHOTOGRAPHIC ASSOCIATES

*2.20c (Below) By Hilda Begay, from the Ray Gwilliam
Collection. These three Teec Nos Pos tapestries (a-c) show the
trend toward combining aniline and vegetal dyes.*
ARIZONA PHOTOGRAPHIC ASSOCIATES

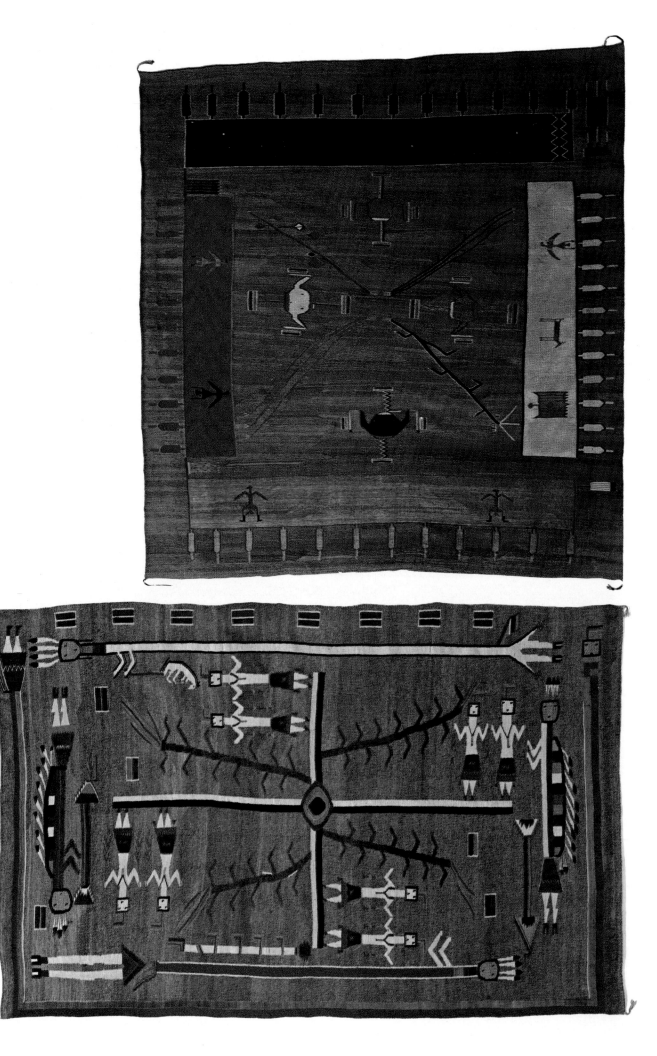

52

2.21 (Left) Hosteen Klah wove this "Shooting Chant" sand-painting tapestry in the early 1920's. The painting represents the white dawn, the blue moon, the yellow (red) sunset, and the black night.
ARIZONA PHOTOGRAPHIC ASSOCIATES
Heard Museum,
Read Mullan Collection

2.22 (Lower Left) Sand-painting rug in the Whirling Log design, from the Harmsen Western Americana Collection, is typical of those woven near Lukachukai about 1925.
ARIZONA PHOTOGRAPHIC ASSOCIATES

2.23 (Right) Woven by Mary Long in 1965, this tapestry is somewhat stylized in both color and design.
ARIZONA PHOTOGRAPHIC ASSOCIATES

2.24 (Below) Yei tapestry in the Shiprock-Farmington style. Colorful Yei figures on a white ground, and fine weaving, are characteristic of the "Shiprock" Yeis.
ARIZONA PHOTOGRAPHIC ASSOCIATES
Read Mullan Collection

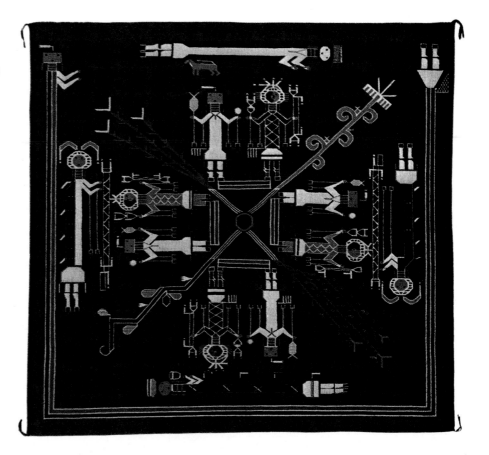

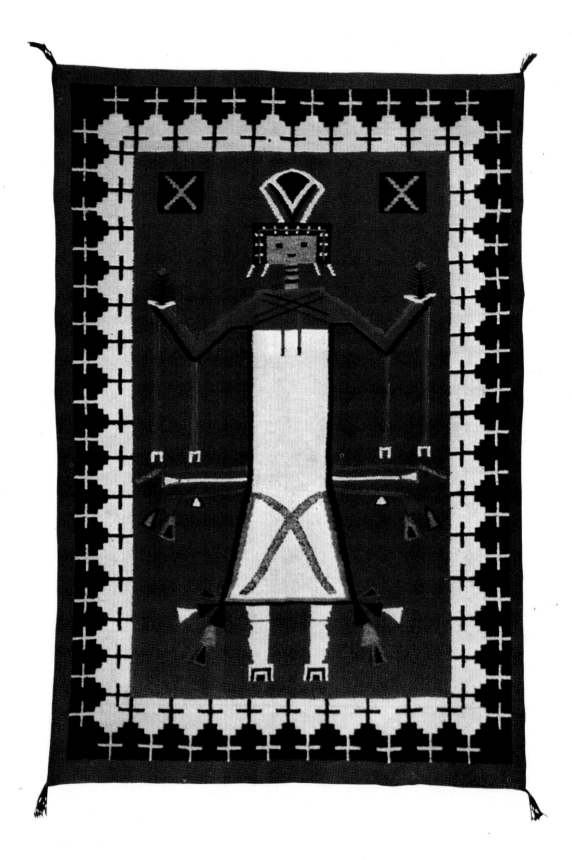

54

At first, only single large figures were depicted, but in time, several Yeis were shown in a row. The development of the Shiprock Yei style is credited to Will Evans, a trader during the 1920's. In this style, the Yei figures are woven in as many as 13 colors, usually on a white ground, and frequently they are framed by a rainbow god around three sides of the tapestry (Fig. 2.24). Sometimes they are completely surrounded by a figured border. Today, most of these are finely woven, often of four-ply commercial yarn.

Yeis are frequently woven in the Lukachukai area, as well, especially around Upper Greasewood Springs. Here, the rugs tend to be larger and heavier than the Shiprock blankets, for they are usually woven of hand-spun yarns. Frequently the ground color is gray, red, or even black, and the Yei figures are larger and less colorful. Usually there is a complete figured border.

Other areas occasionally produced Yei tapestries. Vegetal-dye Yeis are known from Chinle, and the pillow-top and runner weavers of the Gallup area often use such figures on their curio pieces.

Yeibechai rugs differ from Yei textiles in depicting masked dancers performing Yeibechai rites, rather than the Yeis proper. They clearly have human bodies, but they wear masks, square for the female Yeis and round for the male, together with appropriate clothing and

55

ornaments (Fig. 2.26). Earlier Yeibechai rugs depicted the dancers from the front, but more recent ones frequently show most all of the participants in profile, while the leader may face the front or face the line of dancers (Fig. 2.29). All of the areas which produce Yei tapestries also produce Yeibechai rugs in pictorials having the same color patterns.

While they have never been common, pictorial blankets have been a part of the Navajo weaving tradition for a very long time. A few of the early pieces were complete pictures as such (Fig. 2.28), but usually, isolated pictorial elements were incorporated into an otherwise geometric decorative scheme. Many of today's pictorials resemble a catalogue in that they have numerous elements scattered almost at random across the fabric (Fig. 2.27). Others may depict a single motif — simple, as in the American Eagle pictorial (Fig. 2.30), or complex, as in the bird and cornstalk rug (Fig. 2.31). Still others may be fully composed pictures, achieving the kind of unity usually associated with the classic European tapestries (Fig. 2.32).

The beautiful, soft-colored, vegetal-dyed rugs of today are the direct result of the efforts of a few concerned persons. While first Hubbell and then Moore had tried to revive the Navajo weaving of classic times, both had failed, and had produced, instead, the bordered rugs with center motifs. By 1920, most of the rugs being woven were of very inferior quality. At that time, Cozy McSparron, one of the traders at Chinle, encouraged his weavers to return to the simpler striped and banded patterns of earlier times, and to color them with the old Navajo

2.28 Early Pictorial blanket, woven in Germantown yarn, features the railroad train, which had come into the Navajo area only a short time before. Birds and people fill every other space. From Indian Blankets and Their Makers.

2.29 (Below) Yeibechai tapestry in the modern style, with vegetal dyes, woven by Della Woody in 1958. ARIZONA PHOTOGRAPHIC ASSOCIATES *Read Mullan Collection*

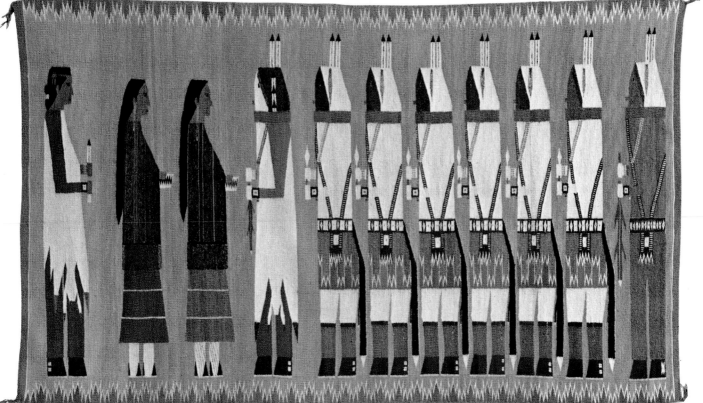

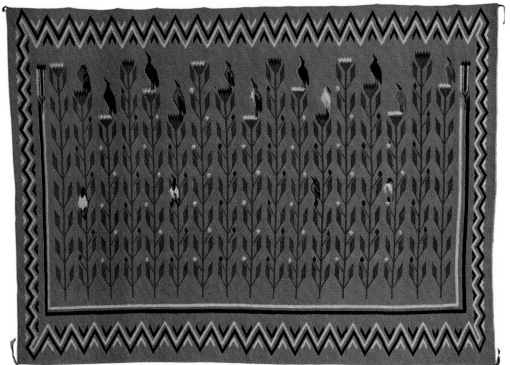

58

2.30 (Far Left) American Eagle pictorial rug, from the Harmsen Western Americana Collection.
ARIZONA PHOTOGRAPHIC ASSOCIATES

2.31 (Left) This Bird-and-Cornstalk rug, woven in 1962 by Alice Ray, was inspired by a very similar rug woven in 1885.
ARIZONA PHOTOGRAPHIC ASSOCIATES
Read Mullan Collection

2.32 (Lower Left) A variation on the bird and cornstalk motif, was woven by Alice Yellowhair in 1968 as a fully composed picture.
ARIZONA PHOTOGRAPHIC ASSOCIATES
Read Mullan Collection

2.33 (Right) Chinle vegetal-dyed rug featuring pastel-colored bands and serrate figures in Late Classic style.
ARIZONA PHOTOGRAPHIC ASSOCIATES
Read Mullan Collection

vegetal dyes, rather than the harsh and garish aniline dyes then in fashion. Mary Cabot Wheelwright, a wealthy patron of the Navajos, offered to purchase their first experimental pieces until a market for these radically different textiles could be established. New vegetal dyes were sought and developed. Today, over a hundred new vegetal dyes are known and used. Special aniline dyes, developed by the duPont company, simulate the soft, glowing colors of the pre-aniline dyes, but these proved too difficult to use, and so other and softer aniline dyes were developed which the Navajo could use themselves.

Fragments of early blankets were found, and tinted photographs of good pieces in private and public collections were made, to serve as patterns for the weavers to follow. It is interesting to note that these models were mostly of the early serrate patterns of post-Bosque-Redondo times, rather than the terraced triangles, diamonds, and zigzags of classic times. By 1930, a distinctive style of rug had evolved. These rugs featured stripes and bands or panels of simple serrate figures, usually in aniline black or red on pastel yellow or yellow-green vegetal-dyed ground. No borders were used. A small but growing market had been established, and the Revival Period was on its way. Today, Chinle rugs are among the finest produced by the Navajo (Fig. 2.33).

Bill and Sallie Wagner Lippincott bought Wide Ruin Trading Post in 1938. Impressed by the Chinle experiment, they encouraged the weavers in the Wide Ruin area to return to stripe patterns and vegetal dyes. New and subtle designs, developed by the weavers, were woven with vegetal-dyed yarns of soft browns, yellows, pinks, and greens. Indigo was reintroduced. Before the Lippincotts left the trading post in 1950, the hand-spun Wide Ruin rug had become one of the most sought-after textiles of the Navajo, and so it remains today (Fig. 2.34a-c).

59

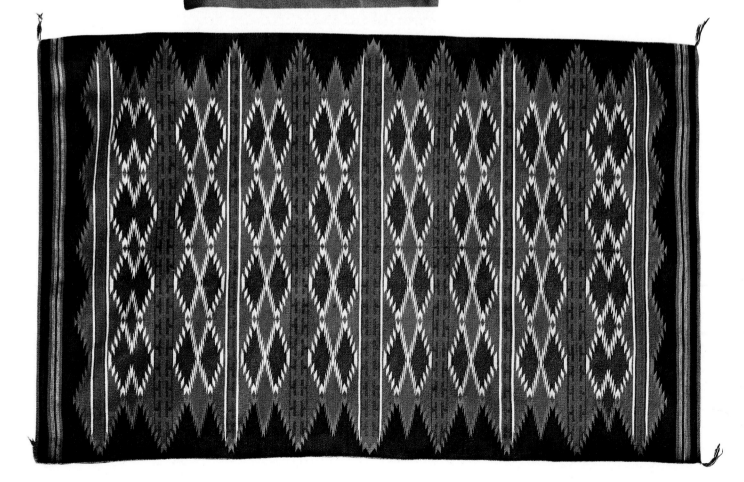

2.34a Woven by Nellie Roan, this Wide Ruin tapestry features vegetal blue color and sophisticated serrate and terraced design elements.
RAY MANLEY STUDIOS
Hubbell Trading Post

2.34b (Below) Modern Wide Ruin rug, woven by Marjorie Spenser, exhibits darker tans and browns, and an unusual serrate design.
RAY MANLEY STUDIOS
Hubbell Trading Post

2.34c (Right) Wide Ruin rug in pastel tans, yellows, and pink, woven by Lottie Thompson in 1960, is typical of the beautifully designed and woven tapestries of the Wide Ruin area.
ARIZONA PHOTOGRAPHIC ASSOCIATES

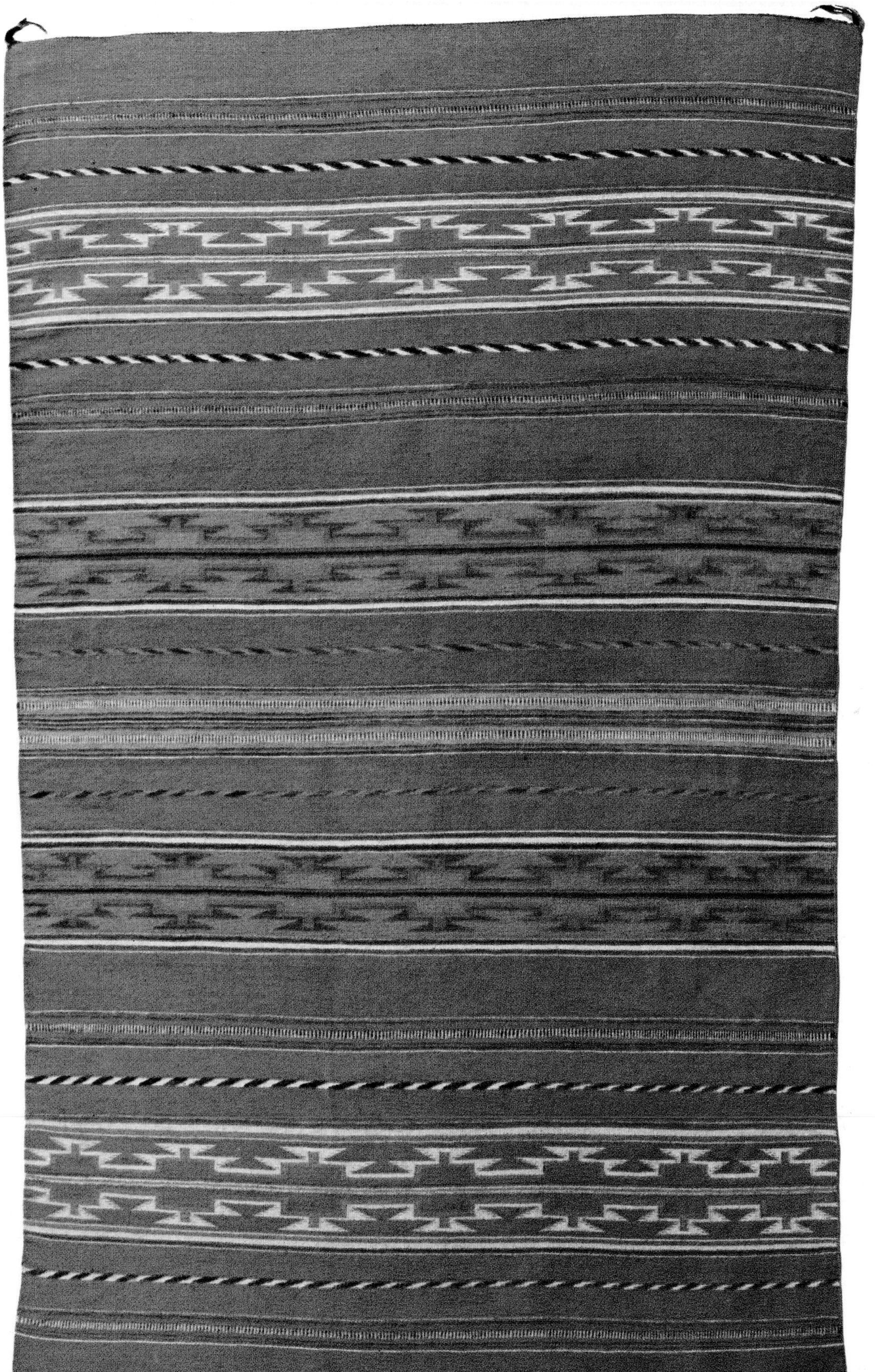

2.35 (Left) The restrained vegetal-dyed colors, and geometric patterns, and the Crystal "wavy" stripe show clearly in this detail.
ARIZONA PHOTOGRAPHIC ASSOCIATES
Read Mullan Collection

2.36 The Ganado Red central motif combined with black, white, and combed gray ground, make this a typical Ganado rug.
ARIZONA PHOTOGRAPHIC ASSOCIATES
Read Mullan Collection

Crystal Trading Post was the next area to adopt vegetal dyes. When Don Jensen went to Crystal in the late 1940's, the local weavers were still producing J. B. Moore Crystal patterns. Before long, native dyes began to replace aniline dyes, and edge-to-edge stripes began to replace the bordered rug with centered pattern. Usually, bands containing simple geometric patterns were spaced on a ground of stripes made by alternating single weft passes with yarns of complementary colors (Fig. 2.35). This technique was used in 1800, but the use of the darker yellows, browns, and earth reds, together with combed gray, lends the Crystal a restrained and pleasing aspect.

While the Revival was going on at Chinle, Wide Ruin, and Crystal, most of the other rug-weaving areas continued to produce aniline-dyed rugs in bordered styles. At Ganado and Klagetoh, the basic design style is very similar. A large, single, elongated, terraced-edge lozenge with appended hooks or terraced triangles, usually occupies the center of the rug, with similar triangular figures at each corner. This central motif is surrounded by a complexly-figured border (Fig. 2.36). Sometimes two, or even more, smaller figures are used in each end of the rug. While white, black, and gray are commonly used in the decoration, the dark, rich red that has come to be known as Ganado Red usually dominates these bold and striking rugs (Fig. 2.37). In recent years, vegetal dyes are sometimes used in combination with the natural and aniline-dyed wools (Fig. 2.38).

One of the most striking modern developments has occurred

2.38 (Left) In this Ganado rug, woven by Marie Begay, the usual gray background is replaced by a vegetal-dyed tan.
ARIZONA PHOTOGRAPHIC ASSOCIATES
Ray Gwilliam Collection

2.39 (Right) Philomena Yazzie wove this fine Burnt Water rug.
ARIZONA PHOTOGRAPHIC ASSOCIATES
Read Mullan Collection

2.40 (Below) This Burnt Water rug, which combines Ganado-Klagetoh design with vegetal dyes, was woven by Maggie Price.
ARIZONA PHOTOGRAPHIC ASSOCIATES
Ray Gwilliam Collection

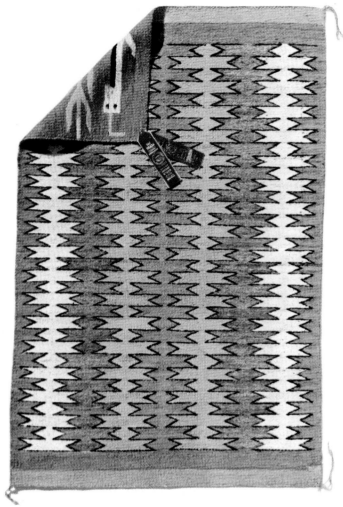

in the Burnt Water area, where fine tapestries have a basic Klagetoh-Ganado design executed in strong, rich, vegetal dyes in deep yellows, browns, earth reds, blues, and greens, occasionally combined with a strong aniline color (Figs. 2.39 and 2.40).

Along the western side of the Navajo Reservation, most of the rugs are still made with borders, and they feature strong geometric figures traditionally executed in red, black, gray, and white. Both serrate and terraced figures are used (Fig. 2.41). The Storm pattern, once centered at Crystal, is now identified with Tuba City. These rugs tend to be more coarsely woven than those of the central and eastern parts of the reservation but still make excellent floor rugs, and the finer pieces tend more and more to be fine tapestries for wall hangings. One recent development in this area is the Coal Mine Mesa raised-stitch outline rug, which basically features simple geometric designs on a background made by alternating weft yarns of different colors in such a way that each color falls on the same warp, thus creating a vertical "beaded" background. Although most of these rugs are made of aniline-dyed yarns vegetal dyes are now beginning to be used.

Twilling or double weave, which once was nearly limited to the weaving of saddle blankets, today occupies a position of its own in

the creation of floor rugs. Patterns have become more intricate, with variations in herringbones and diamonds being woven in fine yarns. Red, black, white, and gray still predominate, but vegetal dyes in browns and yellows are being used more and more. Although many twills are woven throughout the western part of the Navajo Reservation, such twilling is by no means confined to any one area.

Like twills, to which they are technically related, two-face rugs continue to be made in small numbers. Most often, they feature a moderately complex design on the face and a simple pattern of stripes or small geometric figures on the back (Fig. 2.43); but some of today's two-face rugs, however, are marvels of weaving, exhibiting quite complex designs on both the front and the back faces (Fig. 2.42).

In the three centuries or so of its practice, Navajo weaving has served many purposes — as clothing for the tribe and for barter, as souvenirs for the military, as bedrolls and rugs for the American settlers and, later, tourists; and, finally, as superb tapestries for wall hangings. Today, Navajo textiles reflect the cultural contact of many peoples in terms of design styles, materials, and of taste, each modified and adapted by the creative genius of the Navajo woman, who continues to excel in this art.

3.1 *This* Sipikne, *by Alvin James Makya,*
is complete to the last anatomical detail and
outfitted with miniatures of his necessary gear.
RAY MANLEY

3/ Kachinas

by Barton Wright

Huddled on the western promontories of Black Mesa in northeastern Arizona are the small villages of the Hopi Indians (Fig. 3.2). For centuries they have lived there, farming the land below, and for protection building houses of the stone from the mesa tops. These dun-colored walls of native stone, and the recently proliferating cinder blocks, house a people whose artistry is manifested in a multitude of forms.

Few tribes in the Southwest can compete with the Hopi in their production of beautiful crafts. Their basketry has graced homes from California to Colorado for generations. Their textiles have long been traded to all other pueblos in Arizona and New Mexico. The fine silver overlay jewelry they make has been a collector's item for over 25 years, and examples of their superb pottery may be found in most major museums throughout the United States. In addition to these endeavors the Hopi are almost unique in their creation of kachina "dolls."

These "dolls" are brightly colored wooden images adorned with shells, feathers, bits of leather, and other decoration. Their masked faces and costumes are as varied as the fertile imaginations of the Hopi can make them; yet each kachina is dictated by tradition and religion, for these dolls are part of the religious art of the Hopi. The dolls occupy a similar niche for the Hopi craftsman and his religion as do the *santos* for the Spanish-American *santeros* and Catholicism in New Mexico. For the Hopi the carving of these dolls or *kachin' tihu* is but a tiny chip from the log of their religion, yet the same care and attention is lavished upon them as in all other manifestations of their religion. The kachina dolls are but an abbreviation, a condensed symbolization of most of the elements upon which their religion is founded (Fig. 3.3). To understand why kachina dolls are carved it is necessary to take a brief look at the larger complex of the Kachina Cult.

The Kachina Cult is a pan-Pueblo system of rituals and paraphernalia which is necessary for interaction with supernaturals, specifically kachinas. Among the Hopi, every person, male or female, above the age of seven or eight, is a member of this cult. The timing of their initiation into the Kachina Cult is set by the development of their awareness of ceremonial happenings. For the novice, admission into the cult will include initiation by whipping, indoctrination as to the identity and

Editor's Note: The photographs by Jerry Jacka in this chapter are published through
the courtesy of the Heard Museum, Phoenix. They first appeared in KACHINAS: THE
BARRY GOLDWATER COLLECTION, AT THE HEARD MUSEUM, *a book available directly*
from the Museum.

3.2 Sunset on the
First Mesa village of Walpi.
JERRY JACKA

3.3 (Right) Costumes, masks and
symbols indicate the function of
these kachinas to the Hopi.
JERRY JACKA
Barry Goldwater Collection

function of the kachinas, rationalization of their legends, and the beginnings of instruction into the obligations and duties inherent between the kachinas and the Hopi.

The nature and concept of a kachina and the interaction with it is somewhat difficult for the non-Hopi to comprehend, particularly as the Hopi feel it is not essential to organize their supernaturals into categories or hierarchies. Some authors, in attempts at classification of Hopi religion, have characterized the kachinas as ancestral spirits and have equated them with the dead. However, not all dead Hopi are kachinas, nor are all kachinas deceased people. Although kachinas have been called totemic beings, with whom they share certain attributes, their relationships with Hopi clans are different. They are often referred to as cloud people as well as rain deities. Each statement in itself is a partial truth.

Fundamentally, Hopi religion postulates a universe based on a duality of equal but opposite worlds: every visible object in the normal world that has weight and form must have an invisible counterpart in the other world that is formless and weightless. These counterparts are the Hopi kachinas, as infinite in their possible forms as are the objects in the normal world of the Hopi. These kachinas visit the everyday world of the Hopi from January to July, to dance in the village plazas and bring abundance to the Hopi (Fig. 3.4).

The Hopi men who don masks and ceremonial costumes to become these kachinas are believed to be invested by the spirits from the

other world. Through paint, symbols, actions, and attire they give substance to these immaterial life forms, becoming in the process intermediaries between the two halves of the Hopi cosmos. Through this participation in kachina dancing and ceremonies the men keep in close contact with the supernatural.

The Hopi women do not dance nor are they involved in most religious ceremonies and thus have little or no kachina association, which is tantamount to supernatural assistance. To offset this an ancillary system has arisen through time to help the women. Small wooden images patterned after the male dancers but characterizing the kachina spirits are given to the women. These are *kachin' tihu* or kachina "dolls."

These small images have often been termed mnemonic or learning devices through which the Hopi children learn of the specific appearances of the various kachinas, and which helps to keep them in the children's minds during the six months when the kachinas do not appear in the villages. However, this supposition cannot be precisely true, for the dolls are given to the males only when they are babes in arms, while females may receive them all of their lives. As a mnemonic device they serve small purpose, for most boys at the age of six can identify many of the common kachinas, while grown women are often at a loss to do so. Rather than a learning device these small images seem to be an overt prayer for supernatural association and assistance for the women.

The dolls are most frequently given to the younger girls with the number decreasing as they mature. Theoretically, a woman of any

3.4 Against lowering clouds the Crow Mother, standing on the kiva top, epitomizes the appearance of the kachinas.
PAUL COZE

age may receive one. For example, if a woman should desire a child but find that conception is difficult she might request a close male relative to make her a kachina doll. Formerly, this small image would be placed beneath her belt and worn there to promote fertility; undoubtedly the kachina doll that is placed in a cradleboard serves a similar purpose.

The most common function of a doll is to secure supernatural aid in achieving the better things of life such as an abundance of rain, good crops, or possibly protection. Because the women control the food crops and store them in the house which they own, it is only reasonable to keep the dolls there, in close association. The kachina dolls are suspended from rafters and shelves and walls throughout the house like small household deities, but out of the reach of children or possible casual damage (Fig. 3.6). If, however, a girl should want to play with one of the images as a doll she may do so as long as it is treated respectfully.

Infants receive small flat dolls or *puchtihu* (Fig. 3.5), which are hung on their cribs or suspended from the hoods of their cradleboards. The first flat doll given to a baby is usually a representation of Hahai-i Wuhti, the old grandmother, who is keeper of the Hopi Way. She would insure protection for the infant and at the same time set it on the correct path to become a mature and responsible member of the Hopi tribe. The first doll is followed at intervals by several other dolls representing a variety of kachinas. If the infant is a boy other presents will be substituted as he grows older, but if it is a girl she will simply receive more elaborate dolls. *Kachin' tihu* may also be made of monsters or ogres as well as gentler dolls, possibly as a threat or reminder of disciplinary action for imprudent behavior. Dolls of this type, while neither good nor evil in themselves, are a visual prod to recall the capabilities of those supernaturals who are dangerous.

The incredible variety of these images, their symbols, costumes, forms, and functions are the responsibility of the men. It is they who carve the dolls and who present them to the women when they impersonate the spirits in the dances. Any male who has been initiated into the Kachina Cult may carve, but few begin before approximately age 20. They cease to carve only when manual dexterity begins to fail.

The carving of a kachina doll begins with the search and collection of the necessary wood, for only one kind will serve. This is the root of the cottonwood tree. The trunk and limbs of the cottonwood are heavy and obdurate while the root is straight grained and lightweight. It does not split and is easily carved with the most primitive of tools. In addition to these advantages it is a water-seeking wood, an association

73

3.5 These puchtihu *or flat kachina dolls are made for the very young Hopi.*
JERRY JACKA
Barry Goldwater Collection

3.6 (Below) This painting by artist Otis Polelonema depicts the inside of a Hopi house with colorful kachina dolls hanging on the wall.
PAUL COZE

with the supernatural that is of great value to the Hopi with their constant need of moisture to survive.

Despite the fact that cottonwood trees grew in abundance along the arroyos at the foot of the mesas until the late 1920's, it was customary to collect wood at Grand Falls on the Little Colorado River. The wood was stripped of its bark by passage over the falls. The periodic floods of the river brought the wood from upstream and piled it in great windrows in the basin below the falls to dry. Here the wood could be easily selected for size and quality and then be carried on the man's back or by burros to the mesas.

But changes came and the cottonwood trees disappeared from around the mesas; Department of Agriculture edicts declared the tree to be a water-waster and many were cut down near the fields and along the banks of the Little Colorado. An increasing number of the Navajo used the wood for heating, adding to the scarcity of what was never a large supply. By the 1950's some Hopi men were beginning to buy cottonwood roots for a few dollars a pickup load. However, as the wood became increasingly scarce the price rose to $1.50 a running foot by 1965. Today a good piece of wood six to eight inches in diameter and a foot in length may bring a price as high as $20.

The resourceful Hopi extended their area of collecting but never faltered in their demand for cottonwood roots. Aspen wood, which has many similar characteristics, was rejected out of hand. Cottonwood limbs and occasionally that anathema to most Hopi, balsa wood, may be used for a doll, but never if cottonwood root is available to the maker. By 1975 the demand had reached such proportion — with the competition of New Mexican *santeros,* Anglo sculptors, and carvers of imitation kachina dolls — that the wood is being collected, bought, or traded from a vast four-state area.

Once the piece of wood has been selected for the desired doll, a section is removed with a handsaw. The block is then roughly shaped into the figure, using a hatchet, chisels and mallet or butcher knife and a hammer. A variety of wood rasps and knives are then used to work the wood down to where small carved details may be completed, using small pocket knives or carving tools with disposable blades, and fine sandpaper.

In prehistoric times dolls were undoubtedly carved with chips of stone and smoothed with sandstone blocks. However, none of these dolls remains to us. The earliest known doll is in the National Museum in Washington, D.C. It is a Shalako Mana that was collected in the West in 1857 by Dr. Palmer, an Army surgeon (Fig. 3.7). Other early examples, ranging from 1860 to 1890, may be found in the collections of the American Museum of National History and the Heye Foundation in New York City, and in the Museum für Volkerkunde in Berlin.

All of these dolls share a simplicity of carving indicating the use of only a handsaw, knife, and sandstone smoothing block. The arms are tightly folded over the chest and are an integral part of the body. The legs are barely separated by two saw cuts, with little detail worked out and only an indication of the feet. Headgear — such as ears and horns — is often separately carved and attached with wooden pins to the head of the doll (Fig. 3.8).

Today, commercial doll makers carve the arms, kilts, belts, and other appurtenances separately, and then attach them to the body of the doll with white glue and strengthening pegs, rather than search for a root large enough to carve all elements from a single block. If the wood has cracked during drying or if there are imperfections, these are filled with wood dough which is allowed to set and then sanded smooth. The doll is nearly ready for painting.

Cottonwood root must be primed before painting because it is quite porous in structure; therefore it is first given a coat of white clay as a ground. This clay is collected in various locations from the valleys between the mesas, where it occurs in irregular deposits. Large chunks are brought home, broken up, and put in pails of water to soak; this allows the coarser particles to sink to the bottom, leaving only the finer clay in suspension. This creamy clay is then painted on the doll and allowed to dry, effectively sealing the wood and affording a white matte ground upon which to paint details of costume and mask. A few contemporary carvers have begun to use commercial grounds such as gesso

3.7 (Left) First Mesa Shalako Manas.
JERRY JACKA
Barry Goldwater Collection

3.8 The older style dolls are characterized by simple carving and little detail.
JERRY JACKA
Barry Goldwater Collection

or some of the newer acrylic substitutes. This is being done either through an inability to get the traditional material, or in an effort to achieve a greater brilliance in their painting.

The use of color is most important to the carver, for it symbolizes the direction with which the kachina is linked. Because the function of a kachina has a strong relationship with the direction from which it appears, the color is thus a convention for the recognition of identity and purpose of the doll. The Hopi recognize six directions and their associated colors. North is symbolized by yellow, blue-green identifies the west, red the south, and white the east. To these directional colors are added black for the zenith, and all colors or gray for the nadir.

Early native paints were made from oxides of iron, colored clays, vegetable dyes, and copper ores which presented an astonishing array of tones; however, the majority of all dolls utilized less than a dozen of these colors. With the arrival of traders and teachers, army men and other government agents at the Hopi mesas, other paints were introduced. Ink, bluing, watercolors, and oil-base house paints were all tried until their inadequacies became apparent (Fig. 3.10).

When opaque watercolor, or tempera, was introduced, it immediately supplanted every native color with the exception of the beautiful blue-green of copper carbonate which was then unavailable in these new paints. In the early 20th century this shade became available and the final native paint disappeared, leaving tempera the only paint used on dolls. Despite its universal use it was difficult to secure

3.9 The contrast between these two dolls of the Navan Kachina illustrate the trend towards increasing realism.
JERRY JACKA
Barry Goldwater Collection

3.10 (Below) The oil paints used on these old dolls has bled into the white areas with the passage of time.
JERRY JACKA
Barry Goldwater Collection

in the early days, and dolls from the beginning of this century show many substitutions and other efforts at combining paints to achieve a desired color.

For nearly 50 years tempera remained the ideal paint, becoming more satisfactory as different shades and better forms of packaging were introduced. Despite these advantages and the low price, it had one large disadvantage: even when tempera was thoroughly dried it rubbed off on everything. The dolls smeared fingers, shelves, tablecloths, clothes, and even marred each other. In an effort to overcome this difficulty, the Hopi began to experiment with the newly-invented aerosol sprays. In the late 1950's it was not unusual to find a doll whose paint had been "fixed" with anything from hair spray to a charcoal-fixative. Fortunately this period was cut short by the advent of acrylic paints which were easily applied, brilliant in hue, with a long shelf life, and they did not oxidize or rub off. Under numerous brand names acrylics have been steadily growing in use both as a paint and a spray until now they comprise most of the color used.

The final step in completing a doll is the attachment of the costume, with its bits of leather, hair, shells, and cloth. In the selection of these materials to convey realism, Hopi ingenuity is pushed to its utmost. Where the historic carver was content to symbolize an object or simplify the carving of the difficult areas (Fig. 3.11), the modern carver bends every effort to create a realistic appearance (Fig. 3.9). The experienced carver may render every detail in wood or substitute an item from the plethora of Anglo goods that simulates the desired element. An example of this process may be seen in the fir ruff worn about the neck of a kachina dancer, at the base of the mask. Initially, dolls were given a ruff of real fir twigs. The fact that these twigs turned brown and fell off was of little consequence to the Hopi until they began to *sell* the dolls, then it was considered a fault; consequently, Hopi carvers shifted to whittling a ring-shaped lump of wood. The first innovation beyond this was a series of small cuts into the tubular ruff to imitate the irregularity of fir branches. This was followed by the use of several shades of green to further enhance the realism. However, for the painting to be successful it required far too much effort to achieve realism, while chip carving was not realistic enough. This latter technique was finally reduced to a time-saving device that does not appear on the better dolls.

The invention of plastic imitations of conifers led to a rash of figurines with glassy-looking foliage about their necks. These simulations did not really look like miniature branches, and the shiny appearance cheapened the kachina doll. A better substitute turned up, first

79

3.11 The ruffs about the necks of these two Corn Dancers are a very simple indication of the evergreens used by kachina dancers.
JERRY JACKA
Barry Goldwater Collection

from supplies for architectural models, and later in hobby shops in the form of seaweed from the English Channel. When this material was dyed green it resembled, on a miniature scale, the desired foliage and was relatively durable. The final step in this progression has been the use of green yarn. This yarn is cut into short lengths with the ends projecting; when these are stitched together and tied about the doll's neck or ankles, it resembles evergreens more closely than any of the other simulations.

In many instances the materials now used are selected from a world-wide stock rather than the formerly limited local area. Shells, a requirement for many dolls, are no longer secured from the Pacific coast or the Gulf of California but may be supplied through gifts of visitors, donation of collections, from trade, or purchased from the stock of hobby shops and supply houses. A listing of the origin of shells to be found on modern kachina dolls reads like a guide to the shell collecting areas of the world. Cowries from the South Pacific, Turritella from Madagascar, minute and rare shells from Zanzibar or the Caribbean are a far cry from three tiny mesas in the Arizona desert.

Similarly, the Wolf Kachina doll that a generation ago came adorned with the hide and hair of some unfortunate dog is now often attired in mink (Fig. 3.18). The mouse skin used to simulate the hair of a Snake Dancer has given way to sealskin or other substitutes. Tiny, expensive white ermine tails may be used for ruffs or tail pieces of various

3.12 This Soyal Kachina doll wears a miniature cloth wedding robe and yarn bandoleer over his painted kilt and sash.
JERRY JACKA
Barry Goldwater Collection

dolls. Buckskin has been replaced with suede. Even the jewelry worn by kachinas appears, on the modern doll, carefully replicated with minute bits of silver and genuine turquoise. Leather strips with decorated carpet tacks became minuscule concho belts and medicine pouches. Kilts, belts, sashes, and other clothing are made from specially woven cloth, or painted to resemble the actual article (Fig. 3.12). Felt, flannel, grosgrain ribbons, silk and satin all grace the contemporary Hopi kachina doll, gaining in realism what they often lose in artistic merit.

Feathers are essential to most kachina dolls, and their use indicates the function of the figurine. The rain-bringing dolls wear the airy plumes from the breast of eagles or turkeys, indicating the desire for clouds and moisture to aid their crops (Fig. 3.13). The feathers from birds of prey are used on dolls of warriors, guards, and hunters, to link their activities with those of the predators. Warblers, orioles, and many other songbirds furnished feathers indicative of the colors of spring and summer. These traditional associations were religiously followed until recently when the United States Fish and Wildlife Service, Department of the Interior, decided to fulfill regulations governing migratory and protected species of birds. Although prohibited from interfering with the religious use of feathers by the Hopi, an attempt was made to have ceremonial leaders register their use of such feathers with the Service. Because Hopi religion is secretive, little has come of that effort.

*3.13 (Above left) Graceful cloud-like
plumes decorate this Shalako
Mana in a combined visual prayer
for rain and corn.*
RAY MANLEY

*3.14 (Above) Two dolls of
Pookanghoya, the Little War God,
were collected before 1890.*
JERRY JACKA
Barry Goldwater Collection

*3.15 The fan of feathers
surrounding the face of the Sun
Kachina has been carved from wood
to comply with government
regulations.*
PAUL COZE

In compliance with an augmented regulation which protects *all* birds (with the exception of domestic fowl, sparrows, starlings, and pigeons), as well as confusing the output of a handful of commercial kachina carvers with the multi-million-dollar Indian arts and crafts industry, the Service decided to eradicate this minor threat to birds. The result has been an almost total elimination of featherwork on kachina dolls. It is still legal, however, to use most of these same feathers for fishing flies or bed ticking, and non-Indian artists are not harassed for the use of feathers in artwork. Fear of exorbitant fines and stiff sentences that are possible through overlapping state and federal agencies and inconsistencies in the interpretation of the law have driven legitimate dealers and collectors to refuse *all* dolls, and in some instances to sabotage historic artifacts. Doll makers, who are often both religious and commercial artisans, are attempting to carve wooden feathers or substitute ridiculously inadequate domestic feathers (Fig. 3.15). This is a further loss of heritage for the Hopi, and of the aesthetic enjoyment by artists and all others appreciative of native crafts.

Collectors were intrigued with kachina dolls from almost the first moment of American contact. Initially this interest was that of the ethnologist or collector of curiosities with a new and strange culture. These collectors amassed in quantity all of the dolls which they could intimidate the Hopi into selling or trading (Fig. 3.14). The first reluctance of the Hopi to part with every type of doll was soon subverted by individuals, present among all peoples, who either made or sold that which their religion specifically prohibited. The great surge of interest in Indian crafts in the early years of the twentieth century never swept up the kachinas to any great extent. A few individuals continued to collect, but in the main the 1920's are not well represented in the larger collections of kachinas. During the Depression years an occasional collector parted with twenty-five cents to a dollar to purchase a doll that had captured his attention, or a Hopi would take several to town to sell, but the market could not be considered strong.

This is the first period wherein the makers' names became known, for anonymity of craftsmen is the rule rather than the exception among the Hopi. Often these individuals achieved recognition through their association with off-reservation institutions where they were employed as workmen. Certainly this was true of Porter Timeche at El Tovar Hotel in Grand Canyon Village and Jimmie Kewanwytewa at the Museum of Northern Arizona, in Flagstaff.

Jimmie "K," as he was affectionately known to many, became one of the first carvers to sign or initial his efforts, and he did this only at the urging of Mrs. Harold S. Colton, the wife of the founder of the

*3.16 A coyote Kachina doll by the
former chief of Old Oraibi, Tawaquoptewa.*
JERRY JACKA
Barry Goldwater Collection

*3.17 (Right) Several extremely interesting
old dolls by an unknown maker.*
JERRY JACKA
Barry Goldwater Collection

Museum. He was roundly castigated for this by the other Hopi, but despite their disapproval he continued to sign his work from the late 1930's until his death in the sixties.

A few other individuals became known during this period through the uniqueness of their carving. Tawaquoptewa, the old chief at Oraibi, made kachina dolls so unusual that they are easily recognized in any collection (Fig. 3.16). He believed that, as the *kikmongwi* or village chief, he should not make authentic kachina dolls, and yet he needed to have presents for his friends and an occasional doll for a bit of money. His solution was an image with the symbols deliberately changed so that not a single aspect of the doll could be construed as accurate. Otto Pentewa, a carver from New Oraibi, made dolls that were particularly distinctive, for he selected cottonwood roots that were bent or twisted from which to carve dolls. The figures hunch as though in anguish, or twist in apparent effort at dancing. They can only be called caricatures of kachina dolls, yet the humor so often apparent in their carving has made them collector's items. Chief Joe Secakuku, whose small shop in Holbrook was known to thousands of travelers on Highway 66, also carved kachina dolls; however, it is difficult to pinpoint his style, for being a consummate salesman he would claim to be the maker of *any* doll in his shop if it would help the sale.

Occasionally a carver has a trait so distinctive that it enables one to distinguish his work, and yet his name has never become known. One such carver consistently attached the arms and all other free

pieces to the body of the doll by heating small nails and burning a hole through the piece to be attached. The reasoning behind this practice is somewhat obscure since the parts did not move and just nailing the part on would have been much simpler. Unfortunately the vast majority of doll carvers from this period remain anonymous for it was not the custom of collectors to document their acquisitions (Fig. 3.17).

Curiously, even though many of the collectors felt that their dolls might be undesirable "tourist" items and were unable themselves to recognize authenticity when they encountered it, they made no effort to consistently collect from reputable carvers. It is also interesting that examination of collections from this time period produces only a minute number of fakes, yet the literature of the era indicates a great fear of being "taken." Happily for these individuals, the Hopi have never carved dolls to satisfy non-Hopi; rather, the carvings had to reach a certain degree of accurateness or they were ridiculed by other Hopi. Tawaquoptewa seems to have been one of the few exceptions to this but even he was strongly censured for his aberrant dolls. It is still forgivable to omit some details of a kachina, but not to make bogus dolls.

By the end of the 1930's prices had risen to as much as $5 to $10 for a kachina doll, but the approaching conflict destroyed most of the market. During World War II the young men were away and it fell to the older men to keep the crops growing and the ceremonies alive. Travel was virtually nonexistent, and those who dealt in Indian craft items could not reach their source. The result was an almost complete

3.18 (Left) An action doll of a Wolf Kachina poses in a typical dancing position in this carving by Richard Pentewa.
PAUL COZE

3.19 A characteristic group of Kwivi Kachinas, most of them made around the time of World War II.
JERRY JACKA
Barry Goldwater Collection

halt in the sales of Hopi crafts. The decade following World War II was one of recovery marked by the return of veterans who had learned other technologies than tribally-imposed ones. Guilds, cooperatives, and individual craft shops had their inception during this period (Fig. 3.19). Indian events such as the Gallup All-Indian Ceremonial and the Flagstaff Pow Wow began to show Indian-operated booths. Dolls reached a standard price of $1 an inch. The renewed interest brought with it a mildly competitive urge to produce a "better" doll.

Carvers were quick to note that dolls showing a little more movement or action in their stance sold more quickly, and the trend towards "action" dolls began. These carvings were not made in the static traditional posture, but, instead, arms were moved away from the body and the legs bent into dancing postures. Each of these innovations led to another until today heads are thrown back, clowns are carved in contorted positions, arms and legs seem to flail about, and dolls hunch forward in the positions of actual kachinas, often balanced on one toe (Fig. 3.20). Action dolls were not new, for they had been recorded as early as 1892, but it was the beginning of the strong trend towards the contemporary realism of form. The 25-year period from 1950 to 1975 shows a supplanting of the traditional form of dolls, until, at the present, mostly poor or quickly produced dolls are the only ones that can be so classified. Those such as Dick Pentewa, who do carve good traditional kachinas have left the doll in the traditional position with regard to the feet but have moved the arms outward and carved the remainder of the figure in excellent detail.

3.20 *The careful carving and detail of this Eagle Kachina by Alvin James Makya is visible in this photograph.*
RAY MANLEY

3.21 *(Below) The slightly raised head — the positioning of the arms away from the body — the flexing of the leg and foot in mid-stride — all perfectly mirror the poetic beauty of* Angakchina. *The Long-haired Kachina is very popular with the Hopi and their singing and dancing is enjoyed at both night and day dances.*
RAY MANLEY

3.22 The attention to physical detail characteristic of action dolls is very apparent in these two dolls by Alvin James Makya.
RAY MANLEY

Making action dolls brought with it some mechanical problems. Traditional dolls were attached to walls and rafters by strings tied around the neck, where they hung close to the wall in a vertical position. The action doll does not hang well in Hopi homes with its ever-farther-extended limbs and fine breakable details (Fig. 3.21). This, coupled with the desire by non-Indians to stand the doll on tables and shelves, brought about the development of a base. While some carvers, like Sankey George, solved this problem by making the feet large enough to support the figure, others attached the doll to any handy scrap of board which was then either left plain or badly decorated. Through the years these boards have given way to a simple but more elegant slice of cottonwood root for a base and the string tie is slowly disappearing.

By the early 1960's rules for judging kachina dolls took note of the change by including a new category for dolls. These "new" carvers, in their continuing effort towards realism, took note of the details of the human body for the first time. Instead of rudimentary arms, legs, fingers, and torsos, they began to depict these elements with the same care given to costume. Chests developed pectoral muscles and nipples, fingers appeared with fingernails, and physical aspects of every variety were used to enhance kachina dolls (Fig. 3.22). Among the first to consistently carve in this manner were Willard Sakiestewa, Peter Shelton, and his brother Henry. Peter, who was also an accomplished artist, was one of the first to begin using artists' fixatives and acrylic paints. At this time, interest on the part of the general public in Indian objects began to blossom, and kachina dolls were no longer collected by a select few. The result was a dramatic rise in prices late in the decade, with values rising from $50 or $100 to $400 or $500 for the same quality of doll. The lure of these prices produced a flood of additional carvers almost overnight.

Coupled with the new carvers were individual inspirations which became trends or fads in the production of dolls. Some of these

3.23 *A large carving by Henry Shelton of an Eagle Kachina towers over earlier examples of the same doll.*
JERRY JACKA
Barry Goldwater Collection

3.24 *(Below) This complete line of* Ka'e *kachinas was carved as a set. The two other dolls, an Owl Kachina and a* Chuku, *or clown, are not part of the set.*
JERRY JACKA
Barry Goldwater Collection

91

fads were of monetary interest, while others remained in vogue for many years. One which reappears at intervals is the production of jumping kachinas made in the manner of puppets and strung by their hands on crossed strings. When the strings are pulled apart the doll leaps and cavorts about. One of the first individuals to produce these dolls in any quantity was a First Mesa Hopi man named Seeni.

Another development of this same period was the extra-large kachina doll. This trend undoubtedly began when some carver received extra money for a larger carving (Fig. 3.23). Prices are always carefully watched, and to pay extra for a large doll would be incentive enough to start carvers on the spiralling production of ever larger dolls for more money per inch. Quality was not necessarily a part of this swing toward gigantism. One Hotevilla carver produced a doll nearly five feet in height. Another doll, a Palhik Mana in the collections at the Museum of Northern Arizona, is nearly four feet in height. This was not a new concept, for in the same collections there is a doll almost 40 inches in height made during the 1920's. The emphasis on gigantism is a self-defeating direction for carvers, because the market is very limited since few buyers have room to house such carvings. Consequently it was expectable to see a reverse swing toward miniatures. The dolls of some makers slowly shrank in size until they became masterpieces of miniaturization. Mary, Henry Shelton's wife and one of the few women carvers, produced a Rattle Kachina less than ½-inch in height with a completely decorated sash painted on its side. Other carvers, such as Silas and Russo Roy,

*3.25 A procession of
many different kachina dolls emerges
from Coal Canyon.*
JERRY JACKA
Barry Goldwater Collection

*3.26 (Right) Koyemsi emerge from the
Underworld by way of the Grand
Canyon in this imaginative photograph.*
PAUL COZE

Alfred Fritz, and Gene Kewanvuyowma, a 15-year-old boy, are also excellent carvers of miniatures.

The desire to make dance sets, whether motivated by economics or a sense of the incompleteness of a single dancer on a pedestal, produced a minor fad of multiple figures. Precedence for these sets has existed as early as 1900. These early sets are usually of clowns performing their antics on poles, or in pairs, or as partners in a Snake Dance. These have been followed by kachina dance groups such as the Corn Dancers, clown groups (Fig. 3.24), or a procession of different kachina dolls (Fig. 3.25). The final development in this form has been the production of miniature scenes with kachinas artistically placed on driftwood or rocks in the manner of a diorama.

Demands resulting from the influx of collectors have produced several major effects on the doll market, one being the production of clowns. It is not easy to determine whether the demand for clowns is one that has been sparked by the clown as a visual joke or by the inability of the collector to remember the difficult names of the kachina dolls. Certainly the Squash Kachina, *Patung,* is not a clown, yet it is quite distinctive in appearance and is also a great favorite. Being a favorite may be due to the ease with which it can be named and recognized. Whatever the motivation, clowns of all varieties, Koshari (Fig. 3.27), Koyemsi (Fig. 3.26), Chukuwimpkya, Piptuka, or clowning kachinas such as Ho-e (Fig. 3.28) and Kwikwilyaka are the preferred dolls of nearly all collectors. Carvers like Alfred Fritz, Wilfred and Ira Tewawina, Carl

93

3.27 *A Koshari by Henry Shelton is characteristic of*
the humor possible by a good carver in depicting clowns.
PAUL COZE

Sulu, or David Phillips consistently produce hilariously funny carvings whose action and form instantly convey their role in kachina dancing. Many other carvers who specialize in other dolls will on occasion make a clown. Unfortunately this form of carving is having an adverse effect on kachina dolls as a whole, for it appears to be a contributing factor to the lessening variety of dolls carved. Carvers seldom have a repertoire of more than a dozen or so dolls which they consistently carve. To learn the details of a doll that a person has not made before requires that they either see it in a dance, find it illustrated in a book, get another Hopi to describe it, or see it as a doll. Rather surprisingly none of these steps is as easy as it appears, and the result is that any reduction of doll variety has an increasingly adverse effect.

Collectors have inadvertently produced another effect on doll carving by paying exorbitant prices for pornographic dolls. Pornography as such did not exist among the Hopi until a generation ago. The entire Hopi attitude toward sex precluded the necessity. However, when a Kokopelli is produced in all of his correct ithyphallic detail, the non-Indian buys it for a high price and prurient purpose. The Hopi who has no prejudices in this direction will supply dolls which are increasingly pornographic in nature as long as there is a demand. At present there is a good but covert market for this type of doll.

The more innovative of today's carvers have fastened upon another old theme and are producing a far greater number of non-kachina carvings than ever before. Mountain Spirit dancers of the Apache, society chiefs (Fig. 3.29), Snake dancers (Fig. 3.30), women's society participants (Fig. 3.31) and Butterfly or Buffalo dancers (Fig. 3.32) as well as other variants are appearing in quantity. One carver even produces an aberrant doll with a removable mask.

The most recent trend in the manufacture of kachina dolls is the treatment of the doll as an example of fine art. Through time dolls have always suffered attrition as their feathers drooped or became dirty and appendages were broken and their paint dulled. Formerly this was an expectable end for a prayer object and when it was beyond redemption it was discarded and another took its place; it is not, however, an expectable end for an item collected by a non-Hopi as an art object. This attitude has led to a re-consideration of the carver as an artist rather than a craftsman, and in some instances to be considered, rather naively, a sculptor. In actuality it is the application of art market methods of selling kachina dolls, instead of those of the Indian craft market and any basic change in the product.

Alvin James Makya is an example of this approach to kachina dolls. A recognized carver of excellent, realistic dolls (Fig. 3.32 and 3.33), either he or his associates contacted an art gallery and agreed

3.28 (Above) Second Mesa Ho-e clowns as they would appear during the Powamu or Bean Dance.
JERRY JACKA
Barry Goldwater Collection

3.29 (Above Right) An early kachina doll resembling the One Horned Society chief is portrayed with a doll of Sotuknangu in the background.
JERRY JACKA
Barry Goldwater Collection

3.30 Snake Dancers.
JERRY JACKA
Barry Goldwater Collection

3.31 The yellow-faced Lakon Mana stands in front of a Lakon society member who holds her plaque before her in a dancing position.
JERRY JACKA
Barry Goldwater Collection

3.32 (Below) White Buffalo dancers carved by Alvin James Makya.
RAY MANLEY

3.33 This Mountain Sheep Kachina doll carved by Alvin James Makya is characteristic of his carefully executed and detailed carving.
RAY MANLEY

3.34 (Right) Representing a mixed Kachina dance, the procession includes Chaveyo, Kokopelli, Ahote, Hototo, Navan, Heoto Mana, Sikya Chantaka, and others.
PAUL COZE

to furnish kachina doll "sculptures" on the same basis as any other art form. Gallery commissions plus the carver's fee have boosted the prices of these dolls to extraordinary heights in comparison to those received by regular kachina carvers. A few of these carvings have been cast as a numbered set of bronzes for sale at relatively large prices. Unfortunately, the resultant product is a hybrid embodying few of the principles of a good piece of sculpture nor does it fit the necessary requirements of a kachina doll.

Despite the variations noted, most carved kachina dolls remain virtually unchanged. Dolls are more carefully shaped and painted because of access to better technology, but otherwise the bulk of all dolls carved are the equivalent of those made 50 to 75 years ago. There are more carvers than ever before, and a far greater interest in them as individual artists; there is a wider audience to appreciate both the dolls manufactured and the deeper meanings of their function. Carvers now sign their work, and the better craftsmen are sought after for inclusion in collections. Collectors do not try as often to purchase all of the kachina dolls made but tend more toward specialization, attempting to collect a certain kind of doll or the work of a particular carver. Additionally, they search out specific makers, and add to the worth of their collection by documenting both the artist and his village. This insures that carvers such as Emil Pooley, Jeffer Joseph, Anthony Honahni, Gilbert Nasayowma, Larson Onsae, and others too numerous to list will be recognized for their respective abilities. Examples of their work will be preserved not merely for the enjoyment of the non-Hopi but as a lasting tribute to a rich Hopi heritage.

4.1 Among the many notable potters of the Santa Clara Pueblo in New Mexico are Margaret and Luther Gutierrez (sister and brother).
RAY MANLEY STUDIOS

4/ Pottery

by Richard L. Spivey

In 1919, María and Julian Martinez of San Ildefonso Pueblo accidentally discovered the process of firing black-on-black pottery. These highly-polished and artistically executed pieces with their beautifully painted matte designs soon gained a growing market and achieved international recognition for their makers. Thus began the revival of a dying art, an art which gained even wider and more intense recognition beginning in the late 1960's, coincident with what has been called the renaissance of Pueblo Indian pottery of the 1970's.

Pueblo Indian pottery has its roots deep in the prehistoric past. Although today primarily produced as an art form, it has continued a tradition unbroken since ancient times, originating from simple containers made for everyday household use. The knowledge of pottery making probably first came into what is now the Southwestern United States prior to 300 B.C. from northern Mexico. The earliest known pottery in that area was produced by the peoples of the Hohokam Indian culture of southern Arizona, and of the Mogollon culture of southeastern Arizona and southwestern New Mexico. From there the knowledge of pottery making slowly moved northward to the Anasazi Indian culture (approximately today's Four Corners area) but did not achieve artistic excellence until about A.D. 700. By that time major cultural groups were well established, each with a pottery tradition distinct from its neighbors. Women became skilled craftsmen and also skilled artists, for the pottery was painted with designs to make it beautiful. The Mogollon and Anasazi people are probably the ancestors of the present-day Puebloans, while the Hohokam were ancestors of the present-day Pima and Papago tribes of southern Arizona.

The period A.D. 1100-1300 called the Great Pueblo Period, was a time of flowering of the arts; some of the most outstanding pottery of the entire prehistoric period was produced in that era. Outstanding in this great period was probably the Mimbres, a regionally-distinctive Mogollon group, whose "picture pots" have been a great inspiration to many contemporary potters (Fig. 4.2).

Two major factors contributed to the end of the Great Pueblo Period: a serious drought of long duration and the arrival of marauding bands of enemy tribes. Large villages were abandoned as their inhabitants searched for water and for refuge from their enemies. By the time the Spaniards arrived in 1540 the Puebloans had pretty well settled in

their present locations at Hopi, Zuni, Acoma, and the Rio Grande Valley.

The Spanish Period (1600-1800) saw a decline in pottery art. Vessels for Spanish customers were carelessly made; later, metal containers began replacing the handmade pottery at the Pueblos, and still later it became uneconomical for a Pueblo woman to make her own pots when she could barter for inexpensive containers.

It was the coming of the railroads in the 1880's, bringing tourists to the Southwest, that first sparked life into this rapidly-dying art. It became economically worthwhile to make articles for sale as a source of income. Pottery making had always been woman's work, each making her own pots for use in her home. However, into the 1900's the first stages of the art became a specialty of certain skilled people. At first the tourist market encouraged only small pieces, often bric-a-brac such as the brightly painted Tesuque watercolor ware. But when the archaeologists excavating at Sikyatki and Pajarito Plateau encouraged Nampeyo at Hopi (Fig. 4.3) and María at San Ildefonso to work in adaptations of the old styles, the pottery art had new beginnings in excellence. The result was not mere copying. As Bunzel said in 1929 of Nampeyo:

> Nampeyo, a potter of Hano, revived and adapted the ancient ware of Sikyatki. Undoubtedly the original stimulus came from the outside, but it was Nampeyo's unerring discrimination and lively perception that vitalized what would otherwise have been so much dead wood. She did not copy Sikyatki patterns; her imagination recreated the Sikyatki sense of form.

The other potters, seeing the commercial success of María's and Nampeyo's wares, were soon inspired to strive for the same excellence. The dying art began to revive.

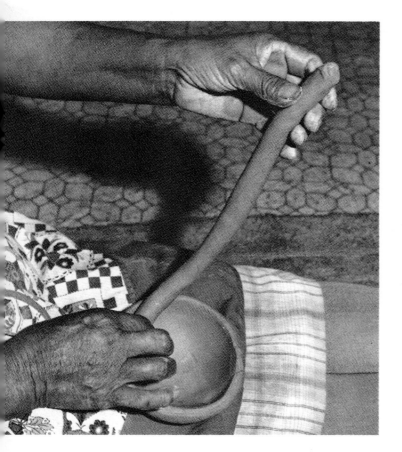

The art of Pueblo pottery making is essentially the same today as it was in ancient times. To quote Lambert, writing in 1966:

> The materials, tools, and techniques of pottery-making . . . in the Pueblos of New Mexico and Arizona . . . do not differ greatly from the material, tools, and techniques used by prehistoric potters of five centuries or more ago. It is true that commercial paints are sometimes used, and there are records of the use of commercially prepared clay by Indian potters. Water color brushes, paring knives, tin cans, scrap iron and other products and by-products of civilization have found their way into the equipment inventory of the Pueblo potter. There are even records of attempts to fire pottery in the oven of a kitchen stove. But for the most part the basic clay is still mined, prepared, molded, decorated, and fired in the traditional fashion. The Pueblo potter of the Southwest has withstood the impact of a non-traditional culture well, and world art is all the richer for that fact.

The clay is dug from deposits near each village. Occasionally potters will go greater distances for the right quality or color. Some potters still offer a prayer in connection with digging the clay, speaking to the earth and asking permission to take the clay, and sometimes leaving an offering. The clay then goes through several stages in preparation: drying, soaking and washing, grinding, sifting, and finally adding temper.

Temper is one of several fine-grained materials added to the clay to reduce shrinkage and cracking in drying and firing. The Tewas

4.6 *Walls are thinned by scraping with a gourd rind.*
JERRY JACKA

4.7 *The paint is applied with a strip of yucca leaf that is chewed to make a brush.*
JERRY JACKA

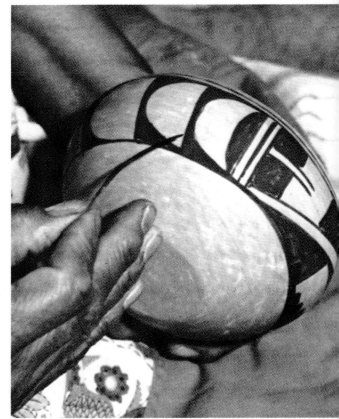

of San Ildefonso, Santa Clara, San Juan, and Tesuque use a fine white volcanic sand commonly called Pojoaque white sand. Zia and Santa Ana pound up basaltic rock; Acoma and Laguna pulverize old pottery shards; while Taos, Picuris, and Hopi usually find no temper necessary. The origin of a pot can often be identified by its temper.

Each potter knows just how much temper to add to her clay. After it is well mixed and contains the right amount of moisture, the potter is ready to begin building her pots.

The traditional Pueblo potter has never known the potter's wheel. Pottery is made by the coil method. Using a *puki* (mold) for a base, ropes of the moist, tempered clay are added one to another until the desired height is reached (Figs. 4.4 and 4.5), then it is smoothed and shaped with a piece of gourd (Fig. 4.6). The pot is then dried, scraped, and sanded for evenness and smoothness. In the case of carved or heavily sculpted vessels, this work is done before the pot is thoroughly dry. The next step is to apply the slip (clay, mixed with water to a creamy consistency) with a rag. Before the slip dries it is either polished with a rag or piece of buckskin, or burnished with a smooth river stone, often to a high gloss. This surface finishing is often the most laborious process in making the pot. After the slipping and polishing, the design is applied with either a brush made from a yucca leaf (Fig. 4.7), or, in the case of more progressive potters, with an artist's brush.

The paints used for the design are either various colors of clay mixed with water, or ground mineral substances mixed with water. To achieve black, either a mineral or vegetable paint is used, depending

105

upon the clay used by that particular Pueblo. For purposes of this discussion, there are two kinds of clay: bentonite and kaolin. Kaolin clay requires a mineral paint (red iron oxide, manganese and iron), which is ground and mixed with water (a little vegetable paint is sometimes added as a binding agent). Kaolin clays are used at Hopi, Acoma, Laguna, Zia, and Santa Ana Pueblos. Bentonite clay requires a vegetable paint made from a spinach-like plant native to the area called *guaco* or Rocky Mountain bee plant. This plant is boiled until it makes a thick paste, is dried, and then stored until needed, then mixed with a little water for use as a paint. In firing, this vegetable paint carbonizes, leaving a black design. Bentonite clays are used at Cochiti, Santo Domingo, San Ildefonso, and traditionally at Tesuque.

Firing is done by building a primitive "oven" in an open area on a dry, clear, windless day. A metal grate is held off the ground, often supported by tin cans, and the pottery to be fired is placed on it, usually upside down. After all the vessels to be fired are placed on the grate, a temporary "oven" is formed by covering the pieces to be fired with large pieces of broken pottery or pieces of tin. The fuel (cedar wood, or cakes of horse, sheep, or cow manure) is then placed under, around, and often over the makeshift oven. The fuel is allowed to burn from two hours to several hours. In the case of Acoma or Hopi the fire is allowed to burn out and the pottery cool before removal from the fire. The black pottery from San Ildefonso and Santa Clara that is so popular is produced by smothering the fire with pulverized manure after about two hours of burning which restricts oxygen from entering the oven. Firing within this reduction-atmosphere causes carbonization, which turns the pots black. In the case of pottery which is not to be black, care must be taken that there is a free flow of oxygen throughout the whole oven area, for a wisp of smoke can leave an unsightly smudge on an otherwise beautiful pot.

The use of assistants in various stages is not uncommon. Husbands often help with the designing; another relative may do the polishing; one potter may even make greenware for another potter, in exchange for a service such as polishing.

There are many shapes being made today by the Pueblo potters. The more traditional shapes are the storage jar, a large globular shaped jar used for storing grain, flour, or bread; the water jar, used for

Utah

Colorado

Arizona

New Mexico

■ Taos

■ Picuris

■ San Juan

Santa Clara ■   ■ Nambe

San Ildefonso ■

■ Tesuque

● Santa Fe

■ Hano

Hopi Towns ■

Jemez ■

■ Zia

■ Gallup

Santa Ana ■   ■ Santo Domingo

■ San Felipe

■ Zuni   Laguna ■   ■ Sandia

● Albuquerque

Acoma ■   Isleta ■

Winslow ●

0   10   20   50   75

Scale in miles

Little Colorado River

Rio Grande River

4.10 These are really fine examples of "María and Popovi" polychromes. The pottery was made by María and the designs were painted by Popovi Da using vegetable black and red clay paint.
RAY MANLEY STUDIOS

storing or carrying water (Fig. 4.8); bowls of various sizes which range from small food bowls to very large dough bowls for mixing enough bread dough for as many as fifty loaves; cooking pots; ceremonial pieces; wedding vases, a double-spouted jar which is used in a wedding ceremony, the bride drinking from one side and the groom from the other; canteens for carrying water; cups and mugs; plates which are forms first made during this century; figurines, some with an ancient tradition and some that are new forms; and ashtrays, for the tourist trade.

Each of the Pueblos has, over the years, developed its own characteristic designs and styles (Fig. 4.9). This diversity is for the most part purely esthetic, for with the exception of only the most recent developments, all current wares are based upon the same technique and have grown out of a common historical background. Experienced potters apply their designs with the utmost freedom, using those retained in their memory and adapted to suit a particular shape, but almost always adhering more or less to a traditional pattern and operating within the limits of an established style.

San Ildefonso traditionally worked in polychrome and black-on-red wares before the black pottery became so popular. The black-on-red ware was red slipped, either stone or rag polished, and with angular and geometric designs painted with *guaco*. The polychrome ware has a grayish-white or cream colored slip, either rag or stone polished, with angular or geometric designs often elaborately detailed and painted with *guaco* and red clay.

Perhaps what might be considered the first development in contemporary pottery was the accidental firing of black-on-black by María and Julián Martinez. Although they continued to work in polychrome, and even on occasion black-on-red, their primary production

108

4.11 Three examples of the early black-on-black by María and Julián Martinez of San Ildefonso Pueblo.
RAY MANLEY STUDIOS

4.12 An early piece of María pottery circa 1925 signed "Marie." The lustrous stone polish without design enhances the beauty and simple classic shape of the pot.
JERRY JACKA

was in black, using traditional designs as well as the more popular feather and water serpent motifs (Fig. 4.11). A red ware was also developed that was essentially the same as the black except that it wasn't turned black during firing. It wasn't until later, when a different and more richly colored slip was sought for the red ware that it was given serious attention.

María was the first Indian potter to begin using her signature on her pottery. By 1926, the idea was beginning to catch on at other Pueblos. María's first signature was simply "Marie" (Fig. 4.12), although there are some early pieces signed with her Indian name, "Poveka." By the early 1930's she was adding Julián's name to the signature, since he did the painting: "Marie and Julián." After Julián's death in 1943 she began working with her daughter-in-law, Santana, and the signature became "Marie and Santana." When she began working with her son Popovi Da in 1956, she changed from using Marie to María and her signature was then "María and Popovi." In the case of pottery *without* design she signed her work "María Poveka." According to Popovi Da, and recently confirmed by Anita Da, she has not made pottery since November or December of 1970, although some pieces were finished later and dated 1971.

Popovi Da, the famed artist and potter son of María, was a perfectionist and great experimenter. For a brief period in the 1960's, working with his mother, he produced some superb polychrome pieces in the traditional manner (Fig. 4.10), like those so well known by Julián and María. During the same period he perfected his gunmetal firing technique, these pieces now being highly sought after by collectors (Fig. 4.14). Essentially it is the same process as for firing black pottery, but with a hotter and longer firing period. The *skill* is knowing when to take the pottery out of the fire; if it is removed too soon it will be ordinary black; if fired an instant too long it will be ruined by overfiring, left with more of a grey color without lustre.

Popovi Da was also the first to develop the two-color firing process that produced black and sienna colors on the same pot (it was a two-*firing* process). For the first firing the pot was fired black in the usual manner; in a second, controlled firing, the black was burned off the desired areas leaving a sienna color. A few pieces were fired so as to turn the whole pot the sienna color. The death of Popovi Da in October, 1971, was a great loss to world art. Also at San Ildefonso, Tony Da — the son of Popovi and Anita Da — was the first to use etching as a method of creating design. After the vessel was polished he would painstakingly and carefully chip off the polished surface with a sharp tool, leaving the design area exposed in a different texture; in the case of red ware, a different color (Fig. 4.13). He was also the first to use turquoise, heishe,

110

4.13 *A traditional shape with the traditional water serpent (avanyu) design but done in the unique style of Tony Da. The turquoise and heishe are added after firing.*
JERRY JACKA

4.14 *Popovi Da gunmetal finish.*
RAY MANLEY STUDIOS

112

and coral on Pueblo pottery. Working with his father during the firing stage, he created beautiful vessels and clay sculptures incorporating these new ideas all in one piece, such as one of his elaborate turtle or bear fetishes fired in two colors with an etched design, and set with turquoise, heishe, and coral, and in the case of a bear fetish, an arrow point tied on the back in the traditional Pueblo manner (Fig. 4.15). His later pieces have become much more elaborate and refined in design (Fig. 4.17) and he has added silver lids to some major pieces.

Also working in the etched style at San Ildefonso are Barbara Gonzales, Tony's cousin, and Tse Pe who works mainly within the framework of Tony's earlier style.

In the late 1960's, Blue Corn and her late husband Sandy began experimenting with a polychrome revival (Fig. 4.16). They first worked with materials and clays traditionally used at San Ildefonso for polychrome pottery and then began experimenting with new clays and pigments. After two years of experimentation they introduced a new polychrome style with a highly polished slip of white, cream, or buff, decorated in elaborate and beautifully executed designs of various colors.

At the present time Gilbert Atencio, the well-known artist, is working on polychrome pieces of traditional materials that promise to be most exciting.

San Ildefonso potters who are currently working in the better known black-and-red ware include Rose Gonzales, Margaret Lou Gutierrez, Helen Gutierrez, Isabel Atencio, Angelita Sanchez, Albert and Josephine Vigil, and María's son and daughter-in-law, Adam and Santana.

Santa Clara has been making black pottery for several hundred years. What was unique about María and Julián's discovery at San Ildefonso was not the firing of black pottery, but the firing of black-on-black — the matte black design on a polished black surface. Traditional Santa Clara wares had undecorated, stone-polished black surfaces, often with fluted rims. The bear paw design, a five-pointed mark that looks like a hand, was commonly pressed into larger pieces. The melon bowl, a vertically ribbed vessel that takes the shape of a ribbed melon or squash, was another traditional form.

Margaret Tafoya, certainly one of the greatest working potters, still works with these traditional forms (Fig. 4.18). She is well known for her traditional water jars, sometimes plain with fluted rims, but more often impressed with the old style bear paw design. She is still able to make the large storage jars decorated with the bear paw design and can build them over three feet high. She works in red as well as black.

Helen Shupla is the only potter still working in the purely traditional melon bowl form. She models thin-walled pots with the melon ribs formed into the walls of the pot itself. These pots are exquisite indeed; they are highly polished, beautifully executed, and well fired. Other potters make an attractive melon bowl form but the ribs are cut out of a thicker pot rather than formed into the finer, thin-walled vessel.

Another type of ware that could be considered traditional at Santa Clara — since it is now in at least its fifth generation — is the unique combination of color and design in the polychrome pottery of Margaret and Luther, a brother-and-sister team (Fig. 4.1). It is known that this type was done by their grandparents and was continued and refined by their own parents, Lela and Van, who worked with eleven colors (Fig. 4.20). It has continued with Luther's daughter, Pauline Narajo, working with Margaret and Luther; and now Pauline's daughter Stephanie is beginning to share in the family secret. After their father's death in 1955, Margaret and Luther continued the work in only seven colors. However, in December 1975 they revived the other four colors, which means the old combinations of colors will be available once again.

4.19 Santa Clara potter Teresita Naranjo produces fine, deeply carved blackware.
JERRY JACKA

4.20 Pottery by Lela and Van that include as many as eleven colors, all of native materials.
PETER BLOOMER

4.21 *Red carved Santa Clara ware by Teresita Naranjo. The rich red slip is stone polished to a high luster while the carved-out areas are painted with an ochre slip and are not polished.*
RAY MANLEY STUDIOS

In the 1930's, two new developments took place at Santa Clara. First was the introduction of the now-famous and popular carved style, both in black-and-red (Figs. 4.19 and 4.21). The second was the development of a polychrome style, a red-slipped pot with designs in yellow, or buff, white, and gray. Santa Clara also works in a black-on-black ware similar to San Ildefonso. Most potters work in these newer styles as well as some of the more traditional ware. Potters at Santa Clara are numerous, but a few of the most noted are Pablita Chavarria and her daughters Elizabeth Naranjo and Mary Singer; Teresita Naranjo and her daughter Stella Chavarria; Belen Tapia and her daughter Anita Suazo; Flora Naranjo and her daughter Frances Salazar; Margaret Tafoya's son Lee Tafoya and daughters Mela Youngblood, Virginia Ebelacker, Shirley Tafoya, and Toni Roller; Santanita Suazo; Ursulita Naranjo; Madeline Naranjo; Angela Baca; Dorothy Gutierrez (miniatures); Nicolasa Naranjo, Legoria Tafoya; Barbarita Naranjo; and, of course, Helen Shupla and Margaret Tafoya.

At Santa Clara, Grace Medicine Flower created an etching process in her own style in the late 1960's (Fig. 4.23). Her earliest pieces were simple, beautifully polished seed bowls with kachina designs etched in various combinations around the shoulder. Working with her brother, Joseph Lonewolf, and father, Camilio Tafoya, she was able to achieve her own two-color firing process, which differs from the one developed by Popovi Da in that it is done in *one* firing, the second color a terra cotta rather than sienna. The reason for the difference in color is that in

117

Popovi's method the black is burned off, whereas in the Grace Medicine Flower and Joseph Lonewolf method, the area never does turn black and so remains more nearly its original terra cotta (or red) color. Exactly how this is done is not known, as potters have always guarded their secrets closely. However, Grace has stated to me that this firing process could have been done by a Pueblo potter five hundred years ago; in other words, the process is not achieved by modern technology but rather as a result of a new but traditionally-based method. Other potters have followed, using a two-color firing process, but to the best of my knowledge, they all achieve the second (sienna) color by burning off the black — *with a blowtorch!*

Grace has grown from her early kachina designs to elaborate, sophisticated, and exquisite (but always original) designs — truly works of art in clay. She is one of the finest of the contemporary Pueblo artists.

Joseph Lonewolf, who did not seriously begin pottery making until 1970, quickly achieved distinction for his "pottery jewels," finely etching Mimbres designs, and experimenting with various colors of clays and pigments. He has worked his pottery masterpieces with sculpted forms, bas relief, and even cameo (Fig. 4.22). Lonewolf and Tony Da have received some of the highest prices ever paid for Pueblo pottery.

Other potters have achieved fame working in the new refined Pueblo technique. Among them are Rosemary Speckled Rock, Lonewolf's daughter, working mainly in exquisite miniatures; and Art and Martha Haungooah, who are increasingly refining their style and originality.

Lois and Derek are producing a new unpolished polychrome type. Experimenting with new colors and reviving old designs, they have executed some fine pieces. Working in a similar vein are Lois' sisters, Minnie Vigil and Thelma Talachy.

Jody Folwell, experimenting with a freer use of clay, is doing some interesting pieces with animal forms in relief. Given a little more time to develop, there is promise she will do some exciting things in design, texture, and form.

San Juan potters worked with plain vessels somewhat like Santa Clara, even firing in black. The lighter vessels were usually red-slipped and stone-polished about halfway down, which would leave the

base a tan color. In black firing, San Juan pottery was often less black in color, and the unslipped base was often grayish in tone. Very little of the old plain pottery is produced today.

In the 1930's, Regina Cata revived a prehistoric incised type which she found on pottery shards from nearby ancient pueblo ruins. A carved polychrome ware has also since been developed. Still working in these types are Tomasita Montoya, Dominguita Sisneros, Rosita Cata, Martina Aguino, and Esther Archulata.

Taos, Picuris, and Nambe use a brownish-colored clay which is filled with tiny particles of mica which show as glittering specks. There is no painted decoration, but the neck is sometimes trimmed with ropes of clay. Small lumps of clay forming knobs may be added for decorative effect, and indentations (punch marks) are sometimes pressed into the pot for decoration. The potters purposely allow fire-blemishes which show as black splotches. The most common form is cookware, as this clay lends itself well to this purpose. Very little is produced at these pueblos today. Virginia Romero of Taos Pueblo is perhaps the best known.

Tesuque used a grayish-cream slip painted with vegetable black. A Greek key design was common. Tesuque's potters early abandoned their traditional form for tourist bric-a-brac, such as the well-known rain-god painted with commercial colors after firing, or, even, painting of designs on sun-dried pottery. Occasionally potters still work on small non-traditional pieces painted with native clay and fired after painting, and even at times fire small black tourist pieces in the style of Santa Clara.

120

4.24 (Left) Storyteller pottery figurines by Helen Cordero of the Cochiti Pueblo in New Mexico. They are as intricate as they are beautiful.
RAY MANLEY STUDIOS

4.25 Traditional Zia water jar by Juanita Pino. Mrs. Pino does very little work at this time as she is well into her 80's.
RAY MANLEY STUDIOS

Santo Domingo pottery is slipped with a fine cream-colored clay usually rag polished. The base is slipped in red and stone polished. The designs are painted in *guaco* and fire a rich black; they are generally either geometric bands of rectangles or squares with corners rounded off, or bird, deer, and floral motifs, occasionally with red added. Santana Melchor and her daughters Crucita and Dolorita are the only potters producing good quality in the old style. A few potters make poorly-fired black pieces or even wares painted with commercial paint, for the tourist market.

Cochiti uses a cream-colored slip (but more grayish-white than Santo Domingo) and usually a stone-polished red base. Designs in vegetable black include clouds, rain and lightning, and human and animal forms that are taboo at other pueblos except for ceremonial pieces. At the present time, Juanita Arquero is producing the better and major pieces in this style.

Bird, frog, and human figures have become increasingly popular at Cochiti. Helen Cordero has become well known for her "Storytellers" of unique charm, and cannot possibly fill in her lifetime the orders she has for these pieces (Fig. 4.24). Other potters who work in animal, bird, and human forms include Seferina Ortiz, Laurencita Herrera, Frances Suina, Virginia Naranjo, Aurelia Suina, Ada Suina, and Mary Frances Herrera.

Zia uses a white or buff slip with the base slipped in red and decorated in mineral black and red, and occasionally a rich yellow. The most common design is a bird circled by a rainbow band (Fig. 4.25).

121

Other designs include deer, floral, and geometric styles. Zia had an early influence at Acoma, particularly on the bird and floral designs, but the Acoma bird is usually more parrot-like. Potters still producing good traditional pieces are Sofia Medina (Fig. 4.26), Dominquita Pino, Eusebia Shije, and Vicentita Pino.

Acoma pottery is slipped in white with the base in red, and painted with mineral black and red, or with black only. The red tone varies from yellow to orange, to red, to dark red. The designs are complicated geometric, and elaborate bird and flower motifs. Bunzel said of Zuni in 1929:

> From all practical standpoints, Acoma ware is unquestionably the best pueblo product . . . The paste is light in color, very fine in texture, and very hard; the surfaces are extraordinarily smooth, the walls of almost eggshell thinness. In spite of the fineness and lightness of the material, the vessels are strong and watertight.

Acoma, along with Zia, produces the pottery most commonly used in the pueblos today.

A strong revival of prehistoric designs began at Acoma in the 1950's by such notable potters as Marie Z. Chino and Lucy M. Lewis. They made wide use of Hohokam designs such as the hunchedback flute player; Mimbres "picture" designs, particularly bird and animal forms;

122

4.26 (Left) This large jar was made and fired in the traditional manner by Zia potter Sofia Medina, and was painted after firing in acrylic paint by her artist husband, Rafael Medina.
JERRY JACKA

4.27 Marie Z. Chino has re-created a prehistoric Mogollon pottery type in this corrugated jar.
JERRY JACKA

and, from the prehistoric cultures, the black-on-white geometric and curvilinear designs of the Tularosa pottery type and the corrugated type which became increasingly and extensively used (Fig. 4.27). The Zuni heart-line deer was borrowed and used in a variety of ways. There is currently a revival of four-color polychromes that have not been done for some fifty years.

Potters of note include Marie Z. Chino and her daughters Rosemary, Grace, and Carrie; Lucy M. Lewis and her daughters Emma and Dolores; Lolita Concho; Jessie Garcia and her daughter Stella Shutiva; Juana Leno; and Mary Ann Hampton.

Laguna clay, form, and design are essentially the same as older Acoma. Unless the origin of the pot is known, it is not usually possible to tell whether it is Acoma or Laguna. Often Laguna pottery tends to be thicker walled and possibly cruder in execution and design. However, there are some fine examples of Laguna pottery, although very little is being made any more.

Santa Ana pottery is slipped in a grayish-white, with a high red base. Designs are red outlined in mineral black, often with bold, crude, thick bands in a terrace formation. Although the last potter, Eudora Montoya, recently held classes teaching other women the pottery art, only small amounts of any importance are being produced today.

Zuni is slipped white with a black or brown base (Fig. 4.28).

123

Decoration is in mineral black, but sometimes with red. The decorated surface is usually divided into four vertical sections, each of which contains a design element such as a rosette, deer, or bird. The neck has a smaller geometric design all its own. Very little of quality has been produced since the 1920's; there are still a few potters working on smaller pieces, such as owls.

Jemez is producing pottery mostly painted with natural-looking colors in commercial acrylic paint, for the tourist market. Earlier, they had made a lot of brightly-colored vessels decorated in poster paint, like Tesuque. There are some recent attempts by a few potters to work in native materials.

Current **Hopi** ware is a result of the Sikyatki revival led by Nampeyo at the end of the last century (Fig. 4.29). Before that time Hopi pottery art had degenerated to the poorest of quality, and designs were greatly influenced by the Zuni tradition. So successful was the revival that by the mid-1920's there was no more of the earlier ware being made.

Hopi slip is the same as the clay body. When it is fired it mottles in color ranging from orange to cream, depending upon the amount of air reaching it. Decorations are in mineral black, reddish orange, and white (Figs. 4.30 and 4.31). They also use a red slip that is decorated in mineral black, and at times, white. The asymmetrical designs are often conventionalized bird forms and feathers, and occasionally

4.28 (Left) Typical Zuni Pueblo pottery from the 1920's. Notice these typical deer, rosette, and rainbird (abstract) designs.
PETER BLOOMER

4.29 (Center) A rare, original Nampeyo from the Fred Harvey Collection at the Heard Museum.
JERRY JACKA

4.30 (Right) The exquisite polychrome vessels in this photo come from the Hopi Arts and Crafts Guild on Second Mesa.
RAY MANLEY STUDIOS

4.31 (Bottom) These examples of the Hopi potter Helen Naha, "Feather Maiden," depict the centuries-old skills of Pueblo artisans.
RAY MANLEY STUDIOS

*4.32 "Frog Woman" Joy Navasie,
in her Hopi cornfield, is surrounded by
outstanding examples of her art.*
RAY MANLEY STUDIOS

kachina forms. A typical Hopi shape is a squat jar with a flattened shoulder and a small mouth. There are two potters of exceptional ability working with the above designs, but with a white slip: Frog Woman, also known as Joy Navasie (Fig. 4.32), and Feather Maiden (Helen Naha).

Nampeyo has many descendants who continue to use her name, and who work with a variety of designs on the yellow clay they consider to be solely their family property. Nampeyo potters include Nampeyo's daughter Fannie and her daughter Elva, and granddaughter Rachel and *her* daughters Dextra Quotskuyva (Fig. 4.33) and Priscilla. Thomas Polacca, Fannie's son, is working with new design forms based on the Hopi tradition.

Other potters include Sadie Adams, Emogene Lomakima, Garnet Pavatea, Beth Sakeva, Verna Nahee, Zella Cheeda, Laura Tomasie, Marcia Rickey, Violet Huma, Lorna Lomakima, Patty Maho, Caroline Talayumptewa, Ethel Youvella, and Grace Chapella, the latter known for her Sikyatki butterfly design. Hopi consists of three mesas. These potters are all from one of the First Mesa villages: Walpi, Sichomovi, the Tewa village of Hano, or Polacca at the base of the mesa.

One Third Mesa potter, Elizabeth White (Polingaysi Qoyawayma), lets the clay "speak to her; she produces pottery vessels freer in form and unique in design, such as corn or flute player motifs in relief with color ranging from creamy white to pink to red (Fig. 4.36). Carlson, writing in 1964, said:

> This extraordinary woman began life in the last years of the last century at Old Oraibi, on the Third Mesa of the Hopi Country in Arizona. Polingaysi Qoyawayma was born in the pueblo that has been continuously occupied longer than any settlement in the United States — more than a thousand years. One of the first Hopi children to receive an education, she was the first of that group to become a teacher. She taught for thirty years in government schools of Arizona and New Mexico. On retirement in 1954, she received a citation and a medal for distinguished service from the Department of Interior. She lives now in New Oraibi, at the foot of the mesa where she was born. . . . She makes prize-winning pottery, reviving the antique Hopi style. . . . She is dedicated to obtaining educational opportunities for Hopi young people.

126

Although not Pueblo, several other Arizona tribes produce pottery. The Navajo produce some brown cookware which is often coated with piñon pitch; today some strictly decorative pieces are made (Fig. 4.34). The Papago produce some crude jars. The Maricopa still make their well-known polished black-on-red ware (Fig. 4.37). A Colorado River tribe, the Mohave, used to be known for their effigy and animal forms (Fig. 4.35); a few effigy-decorated pieces are still made.

There are often questions regarding the symbolism of designs painted on Indian pottery. As Marjorie Lambert has stated (1966): "It is probably safe to say that symbolism of pottery made for ceremonial use is generally understood, at least by village elders, but designs employed only on commercial wares are without meaning, their original significance being forgotten."

Economically, the pottery art of the Pueblo Indian is an important industry. It not only is total support for hundreds of Indian families but is a major part of the income for many Indian art dealers, galleries, and museum shops throughout the Southwest and the world. The Indian potter now makes a good income, and, in the case of the better-known potters, a substantial income. This craftsman no longer works at starvation-level wages like he did just a few years ago. Indian art has met with growing recognition in the world of art, and good pieces are no longer considered curios as they were just a short time ago.

On January 31, 1974 seventeen potters from thirteen New Mexico and Arizona pueblos attended a reception at the White House.

They were invited as artists, as is often done in the nation's capital, but this time they were American *Indian* artists, which illustrates the higher level of appreciation and recognition Indian art now deservedly enjoys.

Pottery art is changing and moving rapidly. Pueblo pottery has never been a static art; it has grown, developed, and changed as society, environment and needs have changed. Underhill stated in 1944:

It is never possible to isolate one product as in "true pueblo style," uninfluenced by Whites or by other Indians. The crafts were and are living arts, developed to fill practical needs. In the course of their history, different phases of each have reached a peak, and there they have paused or dwindled until new materials, new tools, new ideas, or all three, produced a revival. Major changes usually came from the arrival of a different people. The relics show how the pueblos learned first from the south, then from the Spaniards, from the Navajo, Paiute, and Walapai, from the Plains Indians, and from White Americans.

The result was no mere copying, nor is it today. Each new resource was adjusted to the needs of pueblo life and combined with materials and ideas already in use.

Some people are distressed that the pottery being produced today is not the same as it was 100 years ago, but we cannot expect the art to stand still. Today there is much more contact between different tribes, and contact with and living within Anglo society. Ideas are

129

4.35 Examples of the Mohave effigy and animal forms by the noted potter Annie Fields.
PETER BLOOMER

4.36 Some truly fine examples of potter's art by Elizabeth White. The corn designs are in relief on a polished surface.
JERRY JACKA

4.37 *Maricopa Pottery. The tall vase is a unique Maricopa shape inspired by an earlier scalp jar form.*
JERRY JACKA

exchanged and borrowed, as they have been since the beginning of time. We cannot expect a young Pueblo Indian who is as much at home in Las Vegas, New York, Paris, or Tokyo as he is in his own pueblo, to produce the same kind of pottery art, and in exactly the same way as did his grandmother. Needs have changed; ideas have changed; *thinking* has changed. True, most pottery artists are still working within the framework of traditional techniques, but we are seeing the beginnings of new techniques and styles.

Otalie Loloma, instructor, artist, and potter at the Institute of American Indian Art in Santa Fe, expresses her culture and herself in kiln-fired ceramic pottery and sculptured forms. Robert Tenorio at Santo Domingo produces functional stoneware bowls with traditional geometric Santo Domingo designs on a potter's wheel. Also from Santo Domingo, Harold Littlebird builds exciting stoneware pottery forms by the slab technique, employing traditional Santo Domingo geometric, animal, and bird designs, adding his own poetic statement to the vessel.

To be Indian art it doesn't have to be the same as it was generations ago. A non-Indian can make pottery or produce basketry in the traditional Indian style, but that isn't Indian art, it's *copying*. To be Indian art it has to be produced by a person who is culturally Indian, and expresses his culture through his art, whatever the form. If one is of Indian blood, but not of Indian culture, how can he produce Indian art?

Who is to say that an Indian potter cannot use commercial clays, kilns, wheels, or whatever materials or techniques might be available? What is important is that the art be represented for what it is. A pot made of commercial clay, thrown on a wheel, painted with commercial paints, and kiln-fired, cannot be represented as traditional in the sense of materials and technique.

The key is not in how it is done but in why it was done and by whom. If it is executed by an Indian who is validly expressing himself, and through himself his culture, then it is Indian art. To quote a speech given by Popovi Da in Santa Fe for the School of American Research in December, 1969:

We have a form of art which is distinctively North American Indian, but we must preserve our way of life in order for our art to continue.

5.1 *A variety of new and old types of Indian jewelry; for example, the old heshi chunk turquoise necklace styles in the bottom row, center and right of center; the very new silver bead, large chunk turquoise, and silver cone necklace in the upper right; or the old style belt to the left and the new one to the right of center.*

MARKOW PHOTOGRAPHY

5/ Jewelry

by David L. Neumann, and Robert and Sharon Ashton

Making objects of a variety of materials for personal adornment is not a recent innovation among the natives of the American Southwest. Bone, shell, turquoise and other stones, and a variety of perishables including feathers, were utilized for jewelry more than 2,000 years ago in this area. As man became agriculturally oriented and began living a more sedentary way of life, personal adornment became more elaborate and highly prized. In the Southwest, culture in general and jewelry in particular can be more fully studied due to the arid climate which allows perishable objects to better survive.

Following the birth of Christ, Southwestern cultures for the most part can be divided into three major groups: Mogollon, Anasazi, and Hohokam. Each culture in itself is distinctive, yet all share many of the same traditions. All developed pottery, basketry, textile weaving, and jewelry. They established trade with other cultures outside the Southwest, and in some instances trade items such as shell were important in the making of personal adornment.

Perhaps the best known of the three cultures, in innovativeness relative to creative jewelry, were the Hohokam who lived in the south-central and southern parts of present-day Arizona. The Hohokam were best known for their use of turquoise and shell, employing a variety of techniques of working them, including cutting, grinding, polishing, carving, and setting of turquoise in shell mosaic (Fig. 5.2). Shell was also etched with an acid; the final results were exquisite and delicate. Items of jewelry made included pendants, bracelets, rings, necklaces, earrings, and garment ornaments. All techniques except etching and all forms listed were inherited by historic tribes.

By the time Coronado arrived in the Southwest in 1540, the Anasazi, Mogollon, and Hohokam were gone but some descendants

5.2 (Below) In the prehistoric Southwest, turquoise inlay on shell for bracelets, pendants, and other pieces was "high style."
JERRY JACKA

5.3 (Right) A Jemez Dancer wearing a wealth of turquoise, coral, and silver jewelry during the 1959 Gallup Ceremonial.
ESTHER HENDERSON

remained. Where the Hohokam once lived were a people following a relatively simple way of life — the Pima and Papago. To the north and east the Spaniards encountered the descendants of the Anasazi, the Puebloan. Searching for cities of gold they found, instead, cities of earth and stone. These Spaniards noted that the native people with whom they came in contact wore jewelry of various types, most frequently made of turquoise and shell, and that no metals (and certainly no precious metals such as silver and gold) were in use. Within the next few decades, the Spaniards settled in the Southwest, and established contacts that would change forever the way of life for the first inhabitants.

Perhaps a century or so before the Spaniards arrived small bands of Athabascan people wandered into this area. They were hunters and gatherers living off the land. Settling in the Colorado Plateau region in what is now northern Arizona and New Mexico, they began to take and learn much from the settled Pueblo peoples around them. These newcomers came to be known in time as Navajo and Apache.

By the mid-1850's a few Navajo had learned from their Mexican neighbors how to work silver. Before they were removed to Bosque Redondo, New Mexico, in the 1860's, and perhaps as early as the 1830's, there were a few Navajo smiths working with copper and brass. In 1868 the Navajo returned from Bosque Redondo, a defeated and broken people in appearance but not in spirit. The few who knew silversmithing started teaching others and soon the art became a prestigious one among the Navajo people.

5.4 *Handcrafted crosses, usually the work of Pueblo Indians, were popular among the Navajo as well as other tribes. Some of these necklaces included round beads of brass.*
CLOYD SORENSON, JR.

Atsidi Sani, Big Smith, Crying Smith, Smith-Who-Walks-Around, Slim Old Smith, Very Slim Maker of Silver, and Atsidi Clion were some of the better known Navajo pioneering an art form that was to give their people distinction among artisans throughout the world.

The work of the early smiths was highly valued and sought after by fellow Navajo as well as Hopi and Zuni. Objects of silver began to have a great effect upon the lives of all these peoples. Silver jewelry became a symbol of a man's wealth and standing in the community (Figs. 5.3, 5.5, 5.6). A smith was respected and enjoyed prestige given to few others. Those who could afford to own his work were able to display their wealth to the great envy of their fellow tribesmen. This is reflected in the following report in John Adair's *Navajo and Pueblo Silversmiths:*

I asked . . . about the transaction between smith and buyer. He told me: "If a Navajo smith has a bracelet on his arm and another Navajo comes along and sees it, he might say, 'That's a nice bracelet; how much would I have to offer to get a bracelet like that?' The silversmith might say, 'If you like this bracelet how much do you think you could give me? I don't think that you have enough money, you know it is expensive.' Then the other fellow might say, 'I will give you twenty dollars for it.' The silversmith would tell him how long it took him to make it and what a hard job it was. Then he would say, 'I want thirty dollars for it because the materials and the time cost a lot of money.' The buyer will say, 'I will pay you whatever you say because you

know how much it cost you to make it.' The Navajo buying the bracelet would then take it and he would feel proud because he had paid
so much money for it. A smith is doing the Navajo a favor when he
sells him jewelry for a high price because then the buyer can boast of
how much he paid. He wouldn't be able to do this if he sold it to him
for a cheap price. When a smith sells jewelry to a trader it isn't like
that. He sells the silver for whatever the trader offers him for it. He
meets the trader's price. He doesn't care about what the white man
thinks of the silver. Silversmiths stamp designs on the silver which
they sell to the white man that they wouldn't put on the jewelry if
they were selling it to other Navajos. The Navajo won't buy silver
made just any old way."

The second annual report (1880–1881) of the Bureau of
American Ethnology contains a short but significant article written by
Washington Matthews entitled "Navajo Silversmiths," which reflects
some of the early trends in this craft. The opening words are: "Among
the Navajo Indians there are many smiths, who sometimes forge iron
and brass, but who work chiefly in silver." The article illustrates a few
pieces then being produced: a miniature army-style canteen, a few
spherical beads, two simple bracelets, and two powder chargers. A
photograph shows a Navajo wearing a concho belt and a silver bead
necklace with crosses. These crosses were popular with Navajo as well
as other Indians (Fig. 5.4). There is also a plate illustrating the tools
and equipment then in use, including homemade bellows, pliers both
round and flat pointed, molds roughly in the shape of the article to be
made, anvil made from any large metal object or scraps, male and
female dies (for molding buttons), files, scissors, and awls. Simple
indeed were the tools of the first silversmiths.

No piece among the illustrations in Matthews' article has
any setting — turquoise or otherwise. This would seem to support the
contention by Mrs. M. C. Stevenson that the first stones were used not
before 1880. Matthews' text reports that the source of silver was Mexican coins; the source of heat was the charcoal fire, intensified with the
use of homemade bellows, and, for soldering, the mouth-actuated blow-
pipe. The surface of the silver was ornamented by the use of small files
employed as dies; or, as Matthews says, "The other figures were made
with the sharpened point of a file, pushed forward with a zigzag motion
of the hand." This was the language Matthews used to describe the technique known as chasing. This form of engraving has long since been
abandoned by Navajo smiths, and any piece exhibiting the typical mark-
ing of the engraver's tool is probably from the very early days of Navajo
silversmithing.

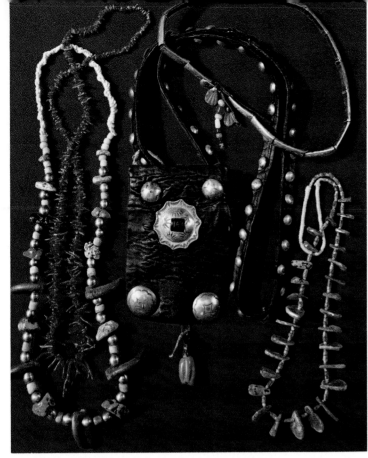

5.7 *Buttons were commonly made of coins and sewed to garments. Here the sleeves and collar of this lady's plush blouse are heavily ornamented with dimes.*

J. H. MC GIBBENY

Silversmithing is not one of the crafts indigenous to American Indians. Its recent origin (going back not more than 125 years) contrasts in time with lapidary work, which extends back through centuries and was well developed in prehistoric (pre-Spanish) times in the Southwest. The present vogue for American Indian jewelry involves both crafts. Silver working, learned initially from Mexican smiths, depends on the availability of that metal, the early source of which was coinage, first American and later Mexican. Silver dimes were ideal for small buttons, while quarters and half dollars were used for larger ones. Some of these buttons required only a little copper loop soldered on the back so that they could be sewn onto cloth (Fig. 5.7). Other buttons were formed by impressing a round of silver (coin or cut-out) into a circular depression; some early photographs reveal their popularity among the Navajo, as they appear on moccasins and pouches as well as clothing. Not to be used as buttons to pass through buttonholes, most were simply ornaments, sewn in rows on velveteen blouses, sometimes hundreds on a single garment. When needed for currency such coins were accepted by traders at their face value, and were, copper loop and all, in common use as ready money.

Before World War I traders had begun to stock one-ounce squares of sterling for the use of Navajo smiths. Much later, sheet silver was introduced to the Indian, replacing both coins and slugs. In earlier years the Navajo "pulled" their own wire, as did other Indians; later it was obtainable commercially. Some of the early silverwork done by Zuni that employed wire was strongly reminiscent of Mexican filigree. Contacts were frequent between Mexican and Zuni when this work became popular. In Santa Fe, there had been commercial production of filigree jewelry in silver, but shortly after 1930 filigree fell out of fashion, the shop making it stopped production, and filigree has not returned to favor to date. Nonetheless, work in wire has remained popular among the Zuni.

Today American Indian jewelry, while still in high favor among the Indians, essentially is made for the "market." It is a commercial production contributing very substantially to the economy of the natives, and also to a large number of dealers. Distribution is now national and organized like any other business. It involves workers and their employers in shops; distributors and jobbers who buy basically from shops in Gallup, New Mexico, but also directly from individual

139

Indians; and traders, who travel nation-wide selling to stores. Thus this trade, like any other, involves retailers, wholesalers, and producers working either in their homes or employed for hourly wages in shops in Gallup and other Southwest communities. Orientation of the market is toward fashions in vogue among non-Indians. Most retail customers live lives unrelated to tribal life styles, and buy and use Indian-made pieces related primarily to current dress styles.

In the early 1970's the most important items were rings, bracelets, and pendants and other pieces worn about the neck, particularly the squash blossom necklace. Earrings were in demand, but pins, until recently very popular, are of less importance today than formerly. And now, in the mid-1970's, the squash blossom necklace has lost its high favor of the early 1970's.

In order to supply the craftsmen, an elaborate business has developed so that there is, throughout the Southwest, an organized supply system involving stores dealing in sheet silver and wire of all gauges and many types. Such silver wire may be of round cross-section, or half-round, triangular, square, or specialty wires such as beaded (Fig. 5.8).

140

5.8 (Left) Bracelets which illustrate the use of a variety of wires, both plain and twisted; such ready-made materials were available and widely used in the 1970's.
TED HILL

5.9 (Right) Coral fetish necklace.
PETER BLOOMER

5.10 (Below) Coral is used in free forms in the bracelet, and in branches in the squash blossom necklace.
RAY MANLEY STUDIOS

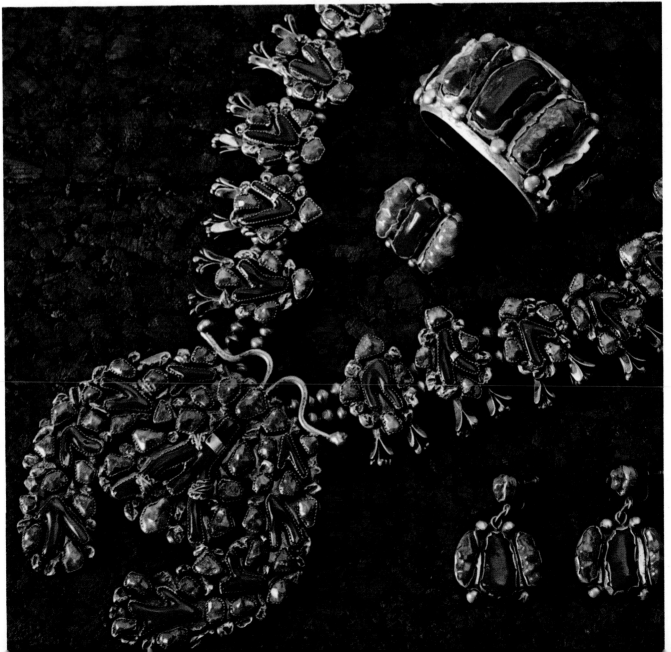

The same suppliers carry turquoise, both rough for the lapidaries (principally Zuni and Santo Domingo) and cut stones for the Navajo who are, typically, *not* lapidaries. Also there are readily-available supplies of tools, both hand and machine types and of modern makes, plus gas torches for soldering. Torches have replaced the gasoline blowtorch which in its day replaced the forge of the first smiths. Forges with bellows were available to the earliest smiths because these silver workers were typically blacksmiths to whom such tools were essential.

Prehistoric turquoise mining was obviously Indian, for there were then no other people in the region. Today, however, no turquoise mining is done by Indians, the turquoise-mining business being entirely in the hands of non-Indians.

Among the materials available to Indian lapidaries in pre-Spanish times were varieties of sea shells obtained through trade, and jet, which occurs in the Southwest (now also imported from England), and native turquoise. These have remained popular to this day and have been added to by dozens of shell varieties from all over the world, plus turquoise from many new Southwestern mines and from Persia. From about 1750 coral beads reached the Southwest from the Mediterranean via Mexico and through import houses of the eastern United States. Today coral is widely distributed in cabochon-cut stones for mounting in silver, in tubular cut beads to be strung and worn about the neck, and in the rough branch forms as taken from the sea (Fig. 5.10). The rough coral branches go primarily to the Zuni, who cut it for use in a variety of ways from inlay in silver, or in shell, to tiny carved animal forms to string for neckwear in so-called fetish necklaces.

Thus, today's Indian smith is dependent upon highly-organized world-wide sources of supply and distribution. Quite a difference exists between the tools and materials of Matthews' time and the present!

For the first forty or so years, Southwestern Indians made objects of silver to adorn and please their fellow tribesmen. The early Navajo work was characterized by massiveness and simplicity. When stones were used, they were few in number and large in proportion to the size of the piece of jewelry. Even Zuni used fewer stones than later on (Fig. 5.11a). But by the turn of the century their craft became popular among the many tourists who were frequent visitors to the Southwest. The Fred Harvey Company (which then introduced significant new

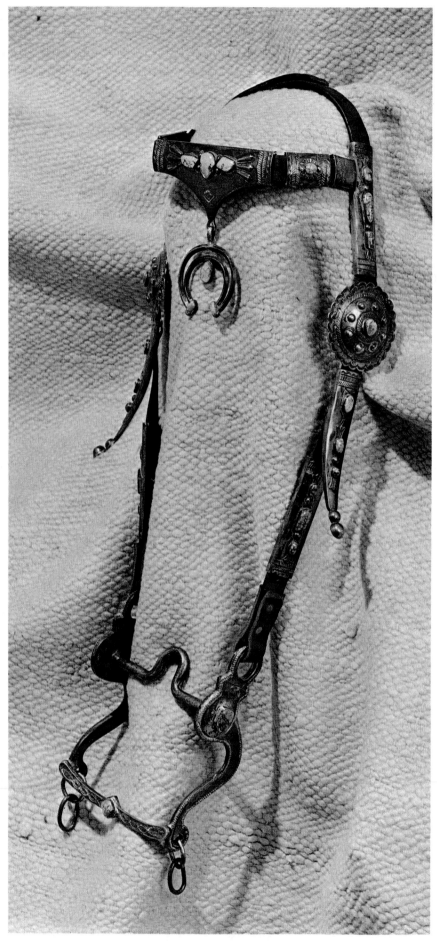

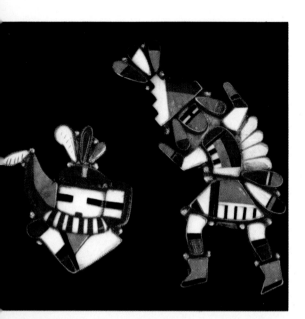

design elements), Lorenzo Hubbell, and Thomas Keams began to merchandise silver bracelets, rings, and the necklace called a "squash blossom" (Fig. 5.12) to people from all over the world. But the Indian continued to make objects for himself and other Indians, especially bridles for horses (Fig. 5.15), concha belts (Fig. 5.32), dress ornaments, bracelets, and necklaces. However, as Southwest Indian jewelry slowly became oriented to the tourists, gradually many of the traditional aspects were lost. During the 1920's, varied designs can be found on the jewelry produced; popular were thunderbirds and swastikas (both introduced at the turn of the century), plus clouds, inverted hands, and others. Some designs may have come from traditional origins, but many were the result of the influence or imagination of the local merchant giving the silversmith designs he felt were "Indian" and would sell. Much symbolism was attached to these designs which were actually White man's ideas and not of Indian origin or meaning.

The year 1910 saw the first manufacturing by machinery of Indian-style jewelry. Manufacturers in Denver, later in Albuquerque, began producing jewelry, some silver, some not, to sell as cheaply as possible to the unwary White tourists. Turquoise began to be much more widely used as it became exceedingly popular, and grades of turquoise that were considered the top became valuable. Old mines reopened and a new market was created for this stone of blue. During the 1920's, 30's, and 40's, the styles of each particular tribe became distinctive, and, in most instances, remain so to the present.

The Navajo had continued their simple heavy silver, usually set with a few turquoise stones (Fig. 5.17). This was also the first style expressed by the Zuni, but gradually they cut their stones smaller and smaller. Partly under the influence of C. G. Wallace, the Zuni also were producing several other different types of work. Using fairly large to very small stones, they developed inlay or mosaic, an old style revived by this tribe. They later began to set small stones which were pointed at each end in separate bezels, and thus created a style called needlepoint which is popular today. A variation on the needlepoint, with one end pointed, one rounded, is often called petit point (Fig. 5.16). Cluster or row work was set with small square, round, rectangular, oval, or teardrop turquoise. Last, and about 1940, the Zuni developed channel work, with stones of *any* shape completely separated from every other stone by a narrow upright band of silver (Figs. 5.13, 5.14).

During this same period, from the 1920's to the 1940's, the Zuni were carving turquoise, shell, and coral into animal-like effigies. Traditionally, animal figurines (called fetishes) were fairly common and were used in religious ceremonies throughout the Southwest for several hundreds of years. The Zuni stylized the idea of a fetish and carved birds and animals small enough to string on necklaces, interspersed with small beads of coral or turquoise (Fig. 5.18). Needless to say, these are neither ceremonial nor symbolic. Leekya Desyee, Quam, Dennis Edaakie, Gordon Leak, and a large number of others became master carvers and silversmiths at the pueblo of Zuni.

Much earlier and continuing to the present, at Santo Domingo and at a few other eastern pueblos, a number of individuals were making and stringing shell disc beads called *heishi;* they were also adding chunk turquoise between groups of shell beads (Fig. 5.19). Up to the 1940's a few Hopi were doing silver work very similar to that of their Navajo neighbors, from whom they learned the craft.

Then, at the end of World War II Fred Kabotie and Paul Saufkie, two Hopis, revived a style of jewelry called overlay which, in the 1930's, had been done by a few of their tribe under the auspices of the Museum of Northern Arizona. Under the direction of these two men, and with the aid of a Federal program, this style of silver work was taught to other Hopi. A silversmithing cooperative was started and today provides an outlet for many Hopi craftsmen as well as being a major source of individual income. Wayne Sekaquaptewa began Hopi Crafts, located on Third Mesa and comparable to what Fred Kabotie and Paul Saufkie began on Second Mesa after World War II. Hopi jewelry utilizes traditional and other designs in the overlay technique. Belt buckles, bola ties, bracelets, concha belts, rings, and many other objects are made by these smiths. This style of jewelry is technically some of the Southwest's finest.

The sudden, explosive passion for Indian crafts in the late 1960's among which silver jewelry and turquoise are leading items, has had its influence on prices, materials, techniques, and designs. As is true in the world at large, gifted, original and innovative designers are not the rule. Among Indians there are, as among all peoples, plenty of competent craftsmen, but when demand exceeds what the competent can produce — as is now the case — a great many inexperienced and temperamentally-unsuited individuals turn to jewelry making for a livelihood. Thus today, along with the considerable production of fine pieces, there

5.18 (Far left) Fetish necklaces made by Zuni Indians. Note the carving on individual figures and the variety of materials: shell, turquoise, jet, coral, and serpentine.
PETER BLOOMER

5.19 A selection of disc bead and chunk turquoise necklaces. These were popular not only with the Puebloan but with the Navajo as well, from early times to the present.
TED HILL

is a mass of inferior jewelry being made by Indians and others in the Indian manner, which is turned out only for sake of profit.

The tools and materials presently available to the Indian smiths, plus an exaggerated market, made it possible to earn so much that the meager earnings of the past are but history. Today Indian smiths ask and readily obtain high prices for their work out of proportion to what equally skilled workers elsewhere can get. This has also encouraged the making of Indian-type jewelry by non-Indians. Today the strands of discoidal beads of shell, heishi, are being very well made in the Philippines and elsewhere, and are imported, distributed, and sold for one-tenth the price asked and obtained by Santo Domingo heishi makers.

Tortoise shell of the hawkbill turtle may no longer be legally brought into this country, this variety having been declared by the U.S. Fish and Wildlife Service to be an endangered species. Tortoise shell had been a material used by the Zuni from the 1940's for inlaying, and by the Domingo for very fine heishi. Pin shell, which can be legally used and is carried in stock by supply houses, results in heishi very similar to tortoise, and has come into wide use.

The terrific inflation in Indian jewelry prices can be illustrated in the following: the two-cent stamp, formerly used to carry one ounce of first class mail, is only a fraction of today's postal rates; this is an extreme, single example of inflation. However, Indian jewelry prices are inflated even more; a strand of Santo Domingo olive shell heishi worth $1.75 to the maker in the 1950's had reached (until the Philippine heishi appeared) a price of $25.00. Note that this was *fourteen times* the old and inadequate price.

Certain Zuni jewelry items have risen equally in price. With very rare exceptions the Indian has been, until today, almost without business experience; nevertheless, the demand for Indian jewelry in recent years has been such that the craftsmen and dealers have asked for and received constantly higher and higher prices.

The handmade silver beads went up and up in price and many of them down in weight and quality (Fig. 5.20). As a result, silver beads machine-made in Albuquerque became popular, particularly as they are

5.20 *Although a well-crafted handmade bead is superior, the majority are rather poorly done; thus, its substitution by machine-made bead is no great loss.*
NEIL KOPPES

often heavier, better finished, and cheaper than common Indian-made beads. However, the very fine handmade bead is a superior piece of craftsmanship and is still made and used on fine Navajo necklaces.

The nature of "handmade Indian jewelry" constantly changes. The earliest efforts (1932) to define it simply followed the then-extant practices: no sheet silver could be used; no rollers could be employed to reduce the melted-down metal into sheets (that had to be done by hammering). But the pieces when finished by the smiths in their hogans could be finally finished by anyone (need not be Indian). Why? Simply because that was the practice. Today much Indian jewelry is finished by the maker who has electric motors and buffing wheels, and *all* smiths use sheet silver from refineries. Hand drawn, very fine tubing (called liquid silver) was formerly made from finely rolled sheet strips and sold for very high prices. Prices became so high that today such hand drawn tubing has been totally driven off the market by equally good machine-made liquid silver.

The familiar heavy "sandcast" Navajo pieces formerly were cast in molds cut in a soft stone (Fig. 5.21). Today these pieces are often cast by the Navajo in cement molds. Tomorrow the extraordinarily efficient centrifugal or lost wax technique will quite probably be adopted by many Indian silversmiths, as some have already done.

The above comments certainly pose the question: what is Indian jewelry? In a summary answer, the following may be said. Where silver is involved it is obviously of recent times, not before 1853. The

5.21 *Cast silver typical of Navajo craftsmen.*
RAY MANLEY STUDIOS

metal itself was of non-Indian origin, first American then Mexican coins. So too were all of the tools and equipment for working silver, with the exception of the few old crucibles of native pottery. Many of the early designs were borrowed from the Mexican leather worker's dies; later designs came from native sources, the tribe producing the object, other tribes, or even prehistoric Indians, or from White men. When turquoise was first introduced to the Navajo it was of Persian origin and already cut in round or oval shapes; most turquoise used today by the Navajo is still cut by others. Later, slugs were substituted for coins, then sheet silver replaced other forms of the metal. New and more sophisticated tools displaced earlier ones, and today some Indians use centrifugal machines. Too, as noted above, beads or objects carved or otherwise prepared in different parts of the Southwest — or of the world for that matter — are combined with items crafted by the Indian himself. What is *Indian* jewelry? Perhaps it is that which is produced by an Indian, regardless of tools or methods.

Too, the questions might be asked: What is pawn? What is dead pawn? There are some doubts relative to the modern interpretation of pawn. Certainly there is, currently, a term misused among those who are interested in this early form of Navajo silversmithing called "old pawn." Originally "pawn" was applied to those objects of silver or turquoise jewelry which were given to a trader in return for credit. If the owner was able eventually to redeem the item from pawn, it would remain his, but if he failed to redeem it, the pawn became "dead." "Dead

pawn" was then offered for sale to anyone who would wish to buy it. Today, anything that is more than three hours old is often misrepresented as "old pawn." "Old pawn" is not necessarily synonymous with *old* and frequently was never *pawned;* however, there are a few examples of *real* old pawn still to be obtained from trading posts and shops throughout the Southwest (Fig. 5.24).

One factor inescapably governing the value of Indian jewelry to a degree is the market price of silver. Silver, a world commodity, is traded on exchanges as are other commodities. Its price through the years has swung from 28 cents a troy ounce (1933) to the high of $6.70 reached in 1974. In 1975 its price has varied from a little over $4.00 to slightly above $4.50. At these prices, heavy large Navajo pieces such as large concho belts which may weigh over 30 ounces have a substantial intrinsic value simply as *metal*.

There is a widespread belief today that turquoise is becoming scarce. This is untrue. More and more turquoise mines have been brought into production in the Southwest, notably in Nevada. The open pit copper mines in Arizona have produced massive quantities of turquoise in recent years — Morenci, Bisbee, Kingman, and Globe. New Mexico, historically the largest producer, particularly at Los Cerrillos, may develop new sources, such as Phelps Dodge open pits at Tyrone. Persia continues to produce as it has for many centuries, and has sent larger and larger quantities of turquoise to this country in recent years. Thus the belief that turquoise Indian jewelry will become scarce is unfounded. Recent production has grown greatly with the ready availability of tools and materials, especially turquoise, and the voracity of the market (Fig. 5.23).

In order to place some perspective on today's prices of Indian jewelry, it may be well to review a particular incident. In the early 1930's a jaunt was made by a trader and a staff member of the Laboratory of Anthropology, Santa Fe, into the Indian country. With a relatively small sum of gift money, the help of the trader who had been buying nothing but pawn and who knew where to get it, and the Great Depression, a wonderful collection of silver was made. The current situation was this. In those years of the early 1930's most Navajo trading posts were in distress and were pressed to pay their wholesale suppliers. The jewelry which they had accepted in pawn was going

153

unredeemed and could be purchased for prices which today are hard to believe. Silver, as mentioned previously, was worth 28 cents an ounce and heavy old pieces could often be had for their value in metal. With that "small gift" the collection made then is to this day the bulk of the Laboratory's collection, and it is one of the best and most extensive now in existence anywhere.

It must be remembered that initially the silverwork of the Navajo was not commercial. Silversmiths worked for themselves, for their personal adornment and that of their families. They made pieces to trade to their neighbors for livestock or other wanted items. Few, if any, relied at first on silversmithing for a livelihood; that is, there were really no professional smiths. Today there are many who make their entire living, or most of it, from silversmithing.

Of recent years the production of silver jewelry among the Hopi has risen to a significant position in the overall volume of work being turned out by Indians. In their post-World-War-II venture, when the Hopi began to develop their own style of work, a considerable number of craftsmen were produced. The silver jewelry of the Hopi must be thought of as an industry, an industry because the work was initiated deliberately as a means of augmenting income. Very nearly all is worked by means of the overlay technique. Overlay is mechanically simple: a solid sheet of silver, usually light gauge, forms the back of the piece, a second sheet of heavier gauge (through which the designs have been cut by the use of a jeweler's saw) is then hard-soldered to the backing. The piece is then oxidized (darkened) and the finishing by some Hopi is accomplished by the use of steel wool, leaving a satin-fine scratch-surface. Very little use is made of stones in Hopi silver whether turquoise or other; however, during 1975 more turquoise than ever before was added to their overlay silver.

Today in the field of Indian jewelry it is the "in thing" to request the name of the smith when purchasing a piece (Fig. 5.25). Many individual Indian jewelers have now achieved prominence in that pieces bearing their names or hallmark have come into demand more for the sake of the known individual craftsman than for the sake of the quality of the piece. Even a few working shops have adopted what might

155

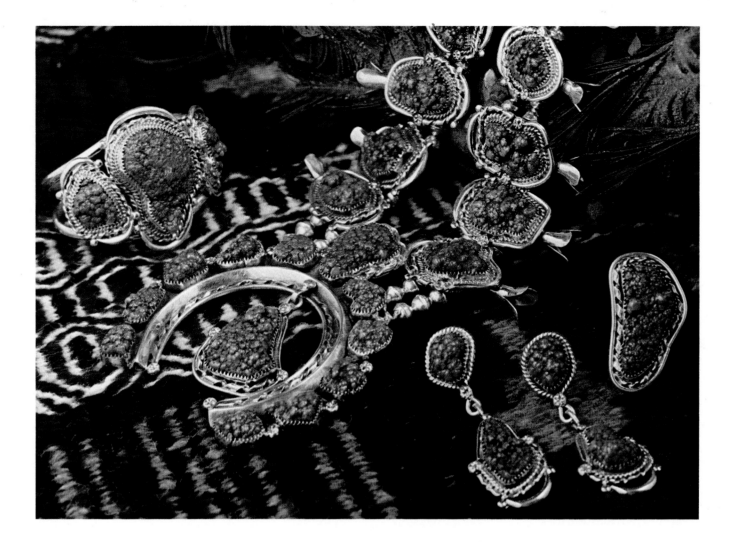

also be called hallmarks, such as the small thunderbird used to mark the pieces of the widely known Thunderbird Shop, or the little outline of a hogan in the center of which the number 3 appears, thus designating the source of the piece as being the Three Hogans Trading Post, to cite two examples. Such pieces, however, commonly do not bear the name of the individual smith.

For several years American turquoise cutters have been cutting stones in free-form only (Fig. 5.26), refusing to cut ovals, rectangles, pear-shaped stones, and the like. This has enabled them to obtain a very much higher carat weight of finished stones from a given weight of rough turquoise than is possible in cutting to the forms mentioned. Many pieces of Indian jewelry require, however, such ovals, rounds, and other geometric forms (Fig. 5.27). Since these shapes are unavailable from domestic cutters, some dealers have been sending American rough turquoise to Persia, Germany, and Hong Kong for cutting, and then importing the finished stones for distribution to suppliers for Indian smiths. This is only one facet of work being done in other countries. Zuni-style fetishes are being made in Italy, Mexico, and elsewhere, imported into this country, and strung and offered to the trade; frequently such fetishes are strung with heishi which is also of foreign origin. What has led to this practice is simple — the excessively high price presently commanded by the work of the Indian jewelers. The foreign cutting of turquoise is in many ways superior to the domestic;

5.26 (Left) Stones cut in free form have been gaining popularity in recent years. Here they are effective as cut in Lone Mountain seafoam nuggets.
RAY MANLEY STUDIOS

5.27 Well matched and well formed cabochon cut stones of Old Burnham turquoise grace this older Navajo necklace. Such stones today are cut outside the United States.
RAY MANLEY STUDIOS

with the exception of the work of the Zuni lapidaries whose work is impeccable (Fig. 5.28), all domestic cutters were non-Indian. One very important point of superiority in the stone cut in Persia or Germany is that they are not backed, but are natural material throughout, that is to say, the rough turquoise has not been treated by heat and chemicals to increase and intensify color and reduce friability of this brittle gem.

The evolution of style in Indian jewelry can be summarized by Navajo changes. Early Navajo work was based on heavy metal, few stones, and relative simplicity of design, as previously noted. With the passage of time and the development of skills and the ready availability of better tools, more delicate work was done, and many stones were used where few had earlier been employed (Fig. 5.29). After Hopi overlay was developed some Navajo adopted this technique, in several instances under the direction of traders. They are very proficient in this style of smithing. Too, it has been mentioned how the Navajo have set Zuni-cut stones in various ways. Slight wonder that one Navajo couple in the mid-1970's is now producing beautiful needlepoint, the man doing the silvercrafting, his wife cutting the stones. The great increase in the price of Zuni work led to the development in Gallup of a series of shops equipped with lapidary tools and manned chiefly by Navajo who are today competing with the Zuni in the production of work formerly attempted only by the latter. Accordingly much work now being done in Gallup is thought to be Zuni because it bears characteristics of the

157

Zuni style, but is, in fact, the work of Navajo. There is good reason why much of the current general Navajo style reflects Zuni influence in the use of a greater abundance of stones.

Obviously Indian silversmithing is in a state of flux, a situation brought about by the fantastically-increased national appetite for Indian jewelry. Many pieces formerly produced completely by Indians are today only *assembled* by them from pre-constructed parts produced by machinery. Among such parts presently being made in machine shops off the reservation are formed squash blossoms, small silver leaves, ring shanks, and most important, the beads previously mentioned. It has long been accepted that machine-made chains used to support pendants did not invalidate the completed article if the pendant had been Indian made. Similarly, the use of manufactured ear wires or posts or clips has long been an accepted practice, as have pin stems and catches, cuff link backs, and the base-metal manufactured backs for bolas now in almost universal use by Indian smiths.

Among contemporary jewelers who are Indians there has yet to emerge a Cellini or Fabergé. There are a few gifted designers whose work has met with recognition. Up to now, all have been limited by a relatively narrow range of techniques. Enameling (whether champlevé or cloisonné), chasing, repoussé, and some other procedures are all foreign to or beyond the range of skills known to the majority of

158

5.28 (Left) Zuni cluster bracelets by the Weebothee family. The members of this tribe cut all stones they use, regardless of shape. These are beautifully matched in form as well as color.
NEIL KOPPES

5.29 More stones were used in Navajo jewelry in later years, as in this necklace with its lovely Old Burnham turquoise.
NEIL KOPPES

contemporary Indian smiths, although chasing and repoussé were both executed by Navajo in earlier years. Among the Zuni certain stone cutting skills have developed to a degree comparable to the best done anywhere by anyone. As yet, and despite growing competition from non-Indians, no one has equaled the skill of the best Zuni cutters of the delicate slender turquoise stones known as needlepoint. However, as with all highly developed techniques, there is an unhappy tendency to produce work merely oriented toward displaying skill. The result has been that some needlepoint-cut stones are so narrow as to destroy the essential nature and quality of turquoise — the color — which is the principal reason for its being regarded as a gem. Larger surfaces than those exhibited by the tiny needlepoint-cut stones are necessary in order to allow the color of the stones to be seen and enjoyed.

Despite all this, there are Southwest Indians who have developed international reputations. Many pieces of jewelry and weaving, devoid of "names," appeared in Europe from the 1930's on. Today the outstanding craftsman is well known by name and frequently in person. Several of these will be cited.

A dwelling which is intimately a part of the sandstone mesas of the Hopi reservation in northeastern Arizona is the workshop and home of jewelry designer Charles Loloma. "I will always bring cultures together," says Loloma. "I have always done this. This is why I do jewelry." Loloma uses a distinctive style and variety of materials from ivory to gold for his individualistic creations in jewelry (Fig. 5.30). His jewelry technically is unsurpassed and his understanding of basic design is equaled by few contemporary artisans. Loloma's concepts of jewelry are considered by many to be the ultimate in tradition combined with a modern form of design.

Loloma began casting simple objects of silver in the early 1950's. Today he works in 14 karat gold and the finest turquoise available. One of his designs adds a striking mosaic of turquoise, shell, and coral on the underside of a bracelet. "A secret only the wearer knows," explains Loloma. His feeling of inner strength is something that does not have to be displayed for all to see. His "height" bracelets and rings are of designs which have emerged gradually over the last two decades (Fig. 5.31, lower center). He is influenced not only by traditional Hopi symbols, but by design and art itself.

Loloma speaks of his work as a "surviving society." "Originality is the essence of what will really survive a culture. When one attempts to copy anyone else, they just may not have the cultural roots to do it. They just don't feel the same way."

The Loloma concept is only one of the new and strikingly innovative designs and styles which are coming alive in the Southwest.

Preston Monongye, a Hopi, is another innovative artisan who is individualistic in his expression and his work. Preston, a master lapidarian and an artist of many media, is well known for his continuing of old combined with new, and he has influenced other Hopi smiths.

There are many individual silversmiths and several that are outstanding, Kenneth Begay, Lee and Mary Yazzie, the Rosettas, Phil Navasya, the Tsikewases, Edward Beyuka, the Reanos, Bernard Dawahoya, and others who are continuing this tradition in their own way.

By way of a few words and accompanying illustrations, one might put his finger on the pulse of what can be seen in the way of Indian jewelry today. Glimpses back in this chapter, and of other pieces from the rich past can be had in the few available pieces of pawn or in old collections. A few examples would include fluted beads and a lovely bracelet style with plain rectangular turquoises flanked by silver drops; single or triple cluster bracelets, some singles edged by double rows of matching turquoise; or a single row of large stones between two triangular silver pieces, with silver drops between stones; old belts, with rounded

5.32 (Left) Classic examples of old style concha belts, with interesting "butterflies" between conchas in the middle example.
RAY MANLEY STUDIOS

5.33 (Top Right) This old style necklace features silver beads between smoothed chunks of Blue Gem turquoise; it has become an inspiration for a variety of more recent pieces.
NEIL KOPPES

5.34 Three regular chunk turquoise necklaces, jacla, and a chunk choker. Left to right, they are from the following turquoise mines: Lone Mountain, Persian, Bisbee (with coral), Fox, and Morenci.
RAY MANLEY STUDIOS

and smooth or punched surface, fluted and stamped surfaces, some with "butterflies" between conchas (Fig. 5.32); old style bridles; Zuni style cluster necklaces; and old Navajo style squash blossoms with fairly plain *najas*. And then there were the Navajo-favored, Santo Domingo crafted, shell disc bead necklaces or with turquoise chunks and complete with *jaclas* (see Fig. 5.19), or perhaps the *jaclas* alone.

Time moves apace and change occurs, slowly or more rapidly. Plain beads become more popular in multiple strands, or they are stamped; turquoise chunk chokers and necklaces are favored (Fig. 5.34), or silver beads are interspersed between smooth and vari-shaped stones (Fig. 5.33). At Zuni all sorts and sundry elaborations occur through the years. Some eliminate the squash blossom on necklaces — or nearly so — with carving or incising of turquoise and shell, combining the two materials in a variety of ways, and using little silver or an abundance of it, the latter with much additional work; leaves of metal became a popular addition, as did flowerlets or the fleur-de-lis theme. Coral in rounded or stem form was combined with other materials; alone or with turquoise it is often crafted in matched sets, which gained popularity into the seventies. Mosaic became more popular and was used in all jewelry forms from old covered shell styles to an elaborate belt combining turquoise and coral with overlay to delicate work in birds or Apache gans

162

dancer figures (Fig. 5.37). Free forms came into focus, either in stones alone or for the shape of the entire piece. A great effort was made to match stones perfectly, either in a single piece or in all pieces of a set. Along with other tribes, Hopi silver became more sophisticated or even more elaborate (Fig. 5.35).

A wide variety of new materials became popular, particularly in the late 1960's and into the 1970's: serpentine, many types of shells from other lands, particularly Africa, gold (Fig. 5.36), pearls, and even animals' claws, "in the real" or cut from some of the materials used such as turquoise. In earlier work except for mosaic, usually one material dominated in a piece of jewelry; in these later years many different stones were combined in a single piece.

Certainly the finest carving of birds, bears, and a few other creatures for "fetish" necklaces preceded the recent period. Nonetheless, today there are well carved and sometimes extremely small fetishes produced by the Zuni. Too, a wide variety of materials may be used in a single fetish necklace, or but one material alone.

Many another trend developed, largely in later years, to add a "new look" to much Indian jewelry. A few of these will be noted. Instead of wire, wider pieces of silver were twisted or rolled and combined with turquoise needlepoint to give a sophisticated look to the end product. More openwork was favored by some smiths. A much larger quantity of Navajo as well as Zuni silver was heavily decorated with turquoise. In some pieces there was a tendency to set stones in individual bezels rather far apart.

Much of the modern jewelry is thus more elaborate, more ornate — yes, even more gaudy — than it was in the past. Nonetheless it still features the basic and lovely combination of silver and turquoise. Many of the fads will pass as they came, fleetingly, but the fundamental beauty of Southwestern Indian jewelry will return and live on.

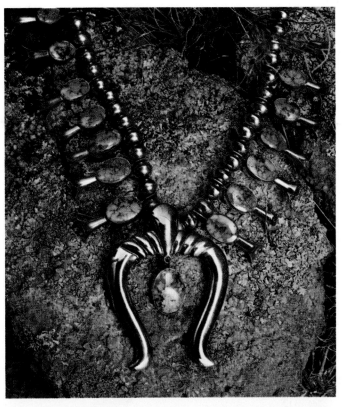